"[Jesus] took her by the hand and said to her, "*Talitha koum!*"
(which means, "Little girl, I say to you, get up!")
— Mark 5:41

Little Girl, Get Up

After suffering a spinal cord stroke Leah
was lifted by her family, her church, the local
community and the medical community

RICK MALWITZ

Rmalwitz@yahoo.com

WESTBOW
PRESS®
A DIVISION OF THOMAS NELSON
& ZONDERVAN

WestBow Press books may be ordered through booksellers or by contacting:

WestBow Press
A Division of Thomas Nelson & Zondervan
1663 Liberty Drive
Bloomington, IN 47403
www.westbowpress.com
844-714-3454

Cover photograph by Jason Denson Photography
http://www.littlegirlgetup.com

ISBN: 978-1-6642-9148-5 (sc)
ISBN: 978-1-6642-9147-8 (hc)
ISBN: 978-1-6642-9149-2 (e)

Library of Congress Control Number: 2023902015

Print information available on the last page.

WestBow Press rev. date: 04/03/2023

DEDICATION

To Donna,
Together, we held hands.
Ecclesiastes 4:9-10

FOREWORD

In a National Football League game the Buffalo Bills were playing in Cincinnati in January of 2023 play came to a standstill when the Bills' Damar Hamlin suffered a cardiac arrest following what seemed to be a routine tackle. As the ESPN broadcast showed Hamlin being taken from the field in an ambulance, I thought of his mom, who would accompany him to the hospital. *She is with him,* I told myself. *That's all that matters.* She would get it done. No doctor, no coach, no teammate loves him as much as she does. At the time I am writing this, Hamlin's mom got it done. Her son is alive and well. He is "recovering." We all are. Damar Hamlin is now a household name. He brought an entire football stadium to its knees, and prayers were answered. We know why. God works miracles.

Leah is my miracle. This is the story of her recovery. It is also the story of Peter and I and her extended family, friends, and the church that loves her. We were all brought to our knees on March 5, 2018, when my oldest daughter suffered a rare spinal cord stroke. We knew there was a God who works miracles.

The first few days and subsequent weeks in the pediatric intensive care at Morristown Memorial Hospital cannot be adequately described in words. (Though my dad will try in this book.) Every so often as I'm straightening up the house after a busy day, I remember the time I left my home with my paralyzed child in a matter of minutes and did not return home for three months. My baby girl needed me and nothing else mattered.

So much of our time at Morristown Memorial Hospital is a blur, but so much I cannot forget, such as the nurse who "accidentally dropped" a few packets of ibuprofen on my lap when I told her I had a headache that first day. I was not a patient and had no dibs on any medicine. Or the child life specialists who went to the store and bought banners and decorations and signs to make Leah's ninth birthday a festive day. Or the doctors, respiratory therapists, and nurses who rushed in to sing "Happy Birthday" to a girl who most certainly had had happier ones.

I will not forget friends who brought me new packets of socks and leggings and tissues with lotion. Or the folks who opened up the Starbucks at five a.m. I loved listening to the nurses who talked of dinner plans with friends and manicure appointments, giving me a much-needed glimpse into the world outside of the hospital walls. I loved listening to their banter. I needed something other than the voices in my head who tended to speak of my Leah perhaps never speaking, eating, walking, or laughing again.

Leah IS a little girl who got up. So many do not. I think of the other families in intensive care who were saying goodbye to their children, just ten feet from where Leah slept. There was a mom in those rooms too.

After one month in the Morristown hospital Leah was transferred to Children's Specialized Hospital in New Brunswick, an amazing place and, I think, a glimpse of the eternal. Children coming alive, caregivers cheering them on, and hugs for all. Leah will often speak of her time there and how nice the nurses and therapists were. That is what she remembers. The wonderful innocence of a child.

When we finally returned home after our hospital stays, it was quite an adjustment. Physically, Leah was by no means the girl she was prior to her stroke, and neither was I. My entire life is now "before," and "after." The after has been wonderful though. So hard, but so good. The first day I dropped Leah off at school her nurse was there waiting patiently at the front door. "Text me when you're close" is what she had said. I tear up just thinking about it. We should all be so lucky to have people who love us like that. I had also written to Leah's principal a few days prior, outlining the necessary adaptations for her school days. Her response? "Whatever you need." I bawled. We were so lucky.

Leah's life is unique. She has scars. She will always have physical limitations. I will always worry about her.

An enduring image of that night at the stadium in Cincinnati is of professional football players on their knees, some of them sobbing, circling the Bills' Damar Hamlin in prayer. Did I pray when my girl went down? Every breath was a prayer. I was honored to accompany her to the hospital on March 5, 2018, and am honored to accompany her today.

My dad wrote a book about his baby girl's baby girl. Thank you for reading.

Abby Malwitz Hansen, February 2023

PROLOGUE

Christianity teaches us that the terrible task has already in some sense been accomplished for us—that a master's hand is holding ours as we attempt to trace the difficult letters. ... And sacrifice in its supreme realisation is not exacted of all. Confessors as well as martyrs are saved, and some old people whose state of grace we can hardly doubt seem to have got through their seventy years surprisingly easily.

—*The Problem of Pain* by C. S. Lewis
Copyright © C. S. Lewis Pte. Ltd. 1940.
Extract reprinted by permission.

Heaven has a special reward for martyrs—Polycarp in the first century, William Tyndale in the sixteenth, and Dietrich Bonhoeffer and Jim Elliot in the twentieth. A confessor, according to the *Oxford English Dictionary*, is "a person who avows religious faith in face of opposition but does not suffer martyrdom."

I have never been a martyr. Or a confessor. I am included in what Lewis would call "some old people."

In February 2018, I reached my seventieth birthday, that biblical three score and ten, and it was, as Lewis offered, surprisingly easy. Fun childhood, wonderful wife, three great kids, five grandchildren, satisfying career in journalism behind me, and a summer home in Ocean Grove, New Jersey, where, in 1956, I made a public profession of faith as the choir behind Billy Graham—a choir that may have even included my mother—sang "Just As I Am without One Plea." Sixty-two years living the Christian life. Easy.

Less than one month later, on March 5, 2018, I attended a spring training baseball game in Clearwater, Florida. Two days after that, I would be going to the airport to pick up my wife, Donna, my brother Nelson, and his wife, Marge. Together we would be attending the Ligonier National Conference in Orlando for three days of intense Bible study. Baseball and Reformed theology. Two of my sweet spots.

I was at a restaurant in Tampa that Monday night when Donna called from our home in New Jersey. As a school nurse, Donna knows when kids ought to be sent back to class, and she could be a tough marker when they are not really sick. I could tell from the urgency in her voice this was different. This was serious.

She was alarmed by how our daughter Abby Hansen explained what was wrong with our eight-year-old granddaughter, Leah, how Leah's body had gone limp for no known reason. Donna urged Abby to take her to the emergency room at Morristown Medical Center. Life was taking an unanticipated turn, and Donna's calls throughout the evening were increasingly alarming.

Abby drove Leah to the emergency room in Morristown, New Jersey, and there they would spend the night. About seven o'clock the next morning, Leah could no longer breathe on her own. A team of doctors, nurses, and respiratory therapists placed her on a ventilator as Abby looked on helplessly, fearing she was witnessing the loss of her firstborn child.

Donna called me early that morning to say it was bad,

making my decision simple: I must go home. I checked out of the hotel and began the drive north on Interstate 95 into the teeth of the worst blizzard of the winter. The ride was punctuated by troubling texts and a disturbing photo from Leah's father, Peter. Leah was attached to tubes and electrodes, her head tilted to the side, her eyes shut. "Don't share this with anyone!" he informed the family.

In medical terms, Leah was "profoundly quadriplegic," unable to breathe … and no one knew why.

Ten days later, we got incomprehensible news. Leah had suffered a spinal cord stroke. Strokes are for people in my demographic, not healthy, athletic eight-year-old girls. About 98 percent of all strokes affect the brain. Fewer than 2 percent affect the spinal cord, like hers. There was no known cause. (There still isn't.) "She won the bad lottery," one of her doctors would tell me.

The short story was that Leah was doing cartwheels in the basement and within twelve hours was paralyzed from the neck down because of something that may have happened down there. "That's what I thought," Leah would say four years later.

But it was not about the cartwheels. If it had been a sudden injury, such as the result of a car accident or a tackle on the football field, the paralysis would have been instant. "If it was caused by something traumatic, you would have seen symptoms right away. Leah's symptoms were evolving, and the issues kept getting worse and worse," said Dr. Michele Fantasia, the director of the spinal injury program and pediatric physiatrist at Children's Specialized Hospital in New Brunswick, New Jersey, where Leah would spend two months rehabbing.

Before the diagnosis, Peter was told not even to look up "spinal cord stroke" on the internet because it is so rare, and Leah was probably suffering from something else. Why worry unnecessarily? Naturally, we Googled *spinal cord stroke*, and the findings were bleak. When Abby looked up the story of a young man who had suffered a spinal cord stroke while in high school and saw how he was in a wheelchair more than three decades later, she immediately closed the link.

Two days later, when she was no longer sedated but unable to speak, Leah mouthed words to her dad. "Am I going to die?" she asked.

"Of course not," Peter told her. Well, of course he said that, though he could not be certain if she would live through those first few days and nights.

The first positive sign of recovery came on the third day. Leah wiggled her right toes. Nerve signals were reaching as far as they could down her body.

After almost four weeks in Morristown, once she was able to breathe on her own, she was transferred to Children's Specialized Hospital in New Brunswick to begin physical rehabilitation. Six weeks after her stroke, she took her first small steps. Eighty-seven days after suffering the stroke, she walked out of the hospital, with a brace on her left leg and a sling holding up her left arm.

She was able to return to the third grade at Millington School for the final two weeks of the school year, accompanied by an aide. Leah was a well-liked girl when this happened, and she was given a hero's welcome. And even though her teacher said she could skip the final math test of the year, she accepted the challenge, took the test, and nearly aced it. "I missed three months of school and got a ninety-eight," she boasted.

Leah would become the cover girl for the Children's Miracle Network of New Jersey and the Children's Specialized Hospital. The head of the hospital would call her "our superstar." She would transform lives.

Physical progress was slow but steady. The next winter, she glided down a bunny slope on skis. The following spring, she used an eleven-ounce bat to play softball. In the fall of 2021, she joined the Central Middle School cross-country team, finishing her first race in thirty-sixth place out of forty, and we were thrilled. That afternoon, Abby recalled how one doctor told her and Peter that Leah might not walk again and certainly would never run again. She ran track in the spring of 2022, with results many might consider weak. We saw it as strong. So did her teammates, who knew Leah's story.

During her recovery, my faith would be challenged as I would grapple with the question, how could an all-loving, all-powerful God allow this? I asked this of many people who have gone through suffering, and the best response came from a believer in Jesus, who had her own physical challenges. "I don't know the answer," she said.

Over the course of Leah's recovery, I would be reminded that the promises of God are true, that suffering has a purpose, that some angels wear green scrubs, that the church is a living being. All the while, I relied on the promise that in heaven, all things will be made new.

Leah's experience prompted my fresh thinking about prayer, the born-again experience, miracles, suffering, and paradise. Today when I read the Bible, hear sermons, listen to podcasts, listen to hymns, and read books, I often put Leah and her recovery story into the narrative, which is how *Uncle Tom's Cabin*, novelist Pat Conroy, actor George Clooney, and Bruce Springsteen will get mentions. Occasionally the narrative will read like the course in Christianity 101 that I imagine teaching as an adjunct professor at a county college, once given the OK to teach what I believe.

One of Leah's final hurdles had been her left arm, which

hung limp at her side for nearly two years, with no movement in her left hand. Her dad called the hand "Lefty," a term of endearment. Then one morning she was able to wiggle the fingers on her left hand. Abby posted the wiggle on Facebook, while in the background she was playing music from *The Greatest Showman*. The video ended with the words "And you see the impossible is coming true."

Abby reported: "And just like that, while we're getting breakfast together and listening to show tunes, Leah wakes up and says 'Mom, look what Lefty can do. It happened last night while I was reading in bed and now, I can do it.'"

Abby and Peter had been told that it might take years for nerves to navigate new paths to her left hand, with growth measured in millimeters. Abby continued in her post: "There are connections being made from brain to nerve to muscle. Tiny and weak yes, but that's all you need. Now repetition, practice, focus and more time."

In those two years, hundreds of people were invested in Leah's recovery: family, church friends, teachers, softball coaches, softball parents, the Girl Scouts, rescue workers, doctors, nurses, therapists, and strangers. Reaction to the breakfast video illustrated the depth of the support from many directions on social media.

"We have been praying for our girl every night, and last night I got to tell the kids how God answers prayer," Kristin Smerillo, a friend from church, posted that morning on Facebook.

"Crying, So beautiful! Go Leah! Thank you God!" wrote Shannon Silverstein, a nurse at Children's Specialized Hospital.

"The most beautiful fingers I've ever seen. Leah—you make my heart so happy!" wrote Cheryl Shanahan, whose son played Little League baseball with Leah's brother Timmy.

"This girl is my hero!!! You go Leah!! I hope to be strong like you one day!!" wrote Kristin Pudlak, the mother of another of Timmy's teammates.

"What a miracle Leah is!!!! How great is this!!!! We will keep praying! Praise God this is happening! What a miracle." wrote Lisa Rosanbalm, one of Abby's college roommates.

"THIS (God working miracles!!!!) is the greatest show!!!! (But the Greatest Showman is incredible!)," wrote Julie Hubner Bearchell, another college roommate.

The breakfast video showed three forces at work: neuroplasticity, a God who heals, and a determined girl.

Neuroplasticity—combining the word neuron, or nerve cell, with plasticity—is the ability of the brain to form new connections, to compensate for injury or disease. Scientists call it "axonal sprouting" when healthy axons sprout new nerve endings to form new pathways to replace damaged nerves. It is like the navigation app on your smartphone that sends you on an alternate path to get around an accident on the interstate.

For nearly two years, Leah had been encouraged to tell her brain to instruct Lefty to "do something." While she was in bed reading that night, Lefty responded.

Prior to the stroke, her brain, her muscles, and her nerves had teamed up to allow her to walk, ride a bike, swing a softball bat, and ski—activities best learned when you are young, and well-learned by Leah. Eight-year-old girls are not yet hardwired, and their bodies are still growing. Her youth and her athleticism have been crucial factors in her recovery. "Now, if that was you, Rick," began one of my doctors, who then dismissed the chances of me recovering with a casual wave of his hand.

It was Dr. Harvey Bennett, of the Goryeb Children's Hospital Division of Child Neurology at the Morristown Medical Center, who had made the diagnosis of spinal cord stroke on Leah's tenth day of hospitalization. When he saw the video, he explained, "Somehow Leah developed compensatory vascular flow to the injured area. The younger you are, the more plastic your nervous system. I think that is why I am in pediatric neurology, because the recovery is much better."

"A young person has much greater capacity for neuroplasticity and recovery relative to an older person. There is debate in the literature regarding what that age is, but absolutely as a child, that is the most favorable prognosis," explained Steven Kirschblum, the director of the Spinal Cord Injury Program for the Kessler Institute for Rehabilitation.

In an email to me, Kirschblum added, "There are recoveries that are beyond what normally occurs in certain individuals. This could be related to 'miracles,' 'belief,' 'religious beliefs and prayer,' 'spirituality,' or a mixture of things including positive attitude, family/social support."

Leah had all the above.

People of strong faith were praying for Leah. There was a strong belief, a positive attitude, and exceptional family and community support. She would be our miracle.

Mark Batterson, author of *The Grave Robber*, based on seven miracles of Jesus recorded in the New Testament book of John, told the *Christian Post*, "Everybody wants a miracle; we just don't want to be in a situation where we need one. You can't have one without the other."

The story is told in the book of Matthew about a paralyzed man brought to Jesus, who was ministering in a crowded house in Capernaum. Unable to bring the man through a jammed doorway, four guys took him to the roof, peeled away the tiles, and created an opening. I imagine the guys holding four corners of an old sail and lowering the man to Jesus, who healed the paralytic.

The story of Leah is a story of help from four corners: the

family, the church, the local community, and the medical community. It has been a perfect storm, on her behalf.

Because of the proximity of both sets of Leah's grandparents, Abby was able to spend eighty-seven days and nights in Leah's hospital room, knowing her other three children were cared for in familiar environments. During the four weeks when Leah was in the Morristown PICU Peter slept in the waiting room. Told by staff he could not sleep there, he slept in his car for as long he could bear the March chill. Timmy, then seven, spent the three months with Donna and me. The four-year-old twins, Serena and Joey, spent the three months with Peter's parents, Art and Ann Hansen.

Liquid Church, where Abby and Peter met during its founding years before it grew into one of largest congregations in the Northeast, offered extraordinary support. So did the community of Long Hill Township, New Jersey, and the hospital staffs in Morristown and New Brunswick, and rebab facilities in Mountainside and Long Hill.

One of the first persons to visit Leah at the hospital was Aimee Pendell Huber, the daughter of Dr. Peter Pendell, the former pastor of Millington Baptist Church, where Liquid Church began in 1999. Abby and Peter were married at the Millington church in 2006. That first Monday night in March, when Leah went to the hospital, Aimee was at a Bible study when someone read an email from Abby. It was very brief and short of details about what had happened. The next day, Aimee visited the hospital and, she would later tell me, "Your daughter was just broken, completely broken."

In a text message to our family, Abby told us about Aimee's visit: "We were talking about how sad this is. Truly, truly sad. But she doesn't want to miss it. You have to be there for the sad, in the trenches, to experience the JOY on the other side. Which is coming."

At the lowest point in her life, when her firstborn child was sedated and completely paralyzed with an unknown illness, Abby spoke of joy. Not just any joy but an all-caps JOY.

CHAPTER 1

This Will Not Be Wasted

In less than two weeks, Leah Rose Hansen would celebrate her ninth birthday. She and her friends would go to a musical at the local high school and then to Leah's house for her first sleepover party. Her father had recently renovated the basement of their home in Long Hill Township, where a dozen or so girls would probably do everything but sleep.

Leah is the oldest of our eight grandchildren, born to our daughter Abby and her husband, Peter. On the day after Christmas in 2017, our son Andrew's wife, Elizabeth Jemison, gave birth to our fifth grandchild, Walter Andrew Malwitz. No matter how many grandchildren we will ever have, I told Leah, "You will always be special. You were the first."

"She was every bit Daddy's little girl that you would imagine," said Peter. "She was such a good sport. I loved having her with me. I loved to ski with her. I coached her softball team."

"She was a dream kid," said Abby. "She was a great student and had tons of fun and lots of friends. You name it, and Leah will do it. She was my firstborn, my best friend."

Leah was active in sports, particularly softball and gymnastics. She was healthy. "I could count the number of sick days on one hand. She often would work through any illness to be part of something," said Abby. Leah loved school.

The first weekend in March 2018 was typical. She played basketball on Saturday, went to Liquid Church on Sunday morning, and then attended a softball clinic in the afternoon. That Monday, March 5, she was dragging a bit and wore her UGG boots to school, knowing she would not be allowed on the floor for gym class. Karen Freeman, the nurse at Millington School, later recalled that she had not seen Leah that day. There were no issues. In the afternoon, she was well enough to play on the playground behind Gillette School, while Abby was inside the school for a conference with Timmy's first-grade teacher.

That night, Peter's mother Ann came to the house to get Timmy and Joey to take them to the Boys Brigade, a program at the elder Hansens' church in East Hanover. Peter would meet the boys there after work and bring them home.

After dinner, Abby was cleaning the kitchen while Leah and Serena went into the basement. "I told them to jump around and have fun. I encourage that." She would tell them to be rambunctious.

Leah called upstairs to tell Abby that her back hurt. Abby told her to come upstairs, sit down, and read a book. After a few minutes, Leah said her hand felt tingly, and then the tingles spread up her arms. Abby told her to go to the first-floor guest room and lie down. But when Leah tried to stand up from the living room sofa, she collapsed.

"'Mom, I can't walk,' she said. I went from not too worried to 'Whoa. This is a pretty big deal,'" Abby remembered.

She called Donna, who remembered, "I received a phone call from my strong, not easily flustered daughter Abby, saying Leah had a bad pain in her neck, and her arms and legs felt very weak." Donna's worst fears were that Leah might possibly have meningitis or encephalitis. She encouraged Abby to take her immediately to the emergency room. Donna called Peter, who was with the boys at church, told him what Abby had said, and insisted he should talk to Abby and convince her to take Leah to the ER.

This did not sit well with Leah, who remembered, "I bawled my eyes out. I didn't want to go to the hospital."

Donna and Peter agreed that Abby should call an ambulance to take Leah to the ER. "I knew we'd get there a lot quicker if I could drive," said Abby.

Leah was deadweight as her mother carried her to her van. (What four-year-old Serena recalled of the drive to Morristown Medical Center was that Leah was laid across the middle seat of the van and did not wear a seat belt, violating a strict family rule.) Peter met them outside the ER and carried Leah inside. It was flu season, and the ER was crowded with kids. "In the back of my head, I'm thinking, *She has some kind of odd flu virus, and we'll check this out,*" said Abby. "*I hope this doesn't become a thing. This better be quick.*"

Leah remembered being in the ER for more than two hours before she was seen by a doctor. "My mom kept going to the [check-in] window—the poor woman behind the window—and being very pushy. 'Let's move this along.'"

Eventually, Leah was given a CT scan and x-rays, and doctors were stumped, unable to explain the paralysis. At about three o'clock in the morning, Peter left the hospital to go to the house in Long Hill where Abby's sister Carrie was watching the other three kids. "Leah was kind of OK when I left," said Peter.

Abby and Leah remained in the ER, and for several hours, the two of them slept together in a bed in the hallway outside the ER. Abby recalled, "We woke up at about six thirty, and I said, 'Good morning, honey. How are you doing?' She said it was very stuffy. I fanned her off, hoping it would revive her a bit. Then she said, 'Mom, I can't breathe.'

"I found a nurse—and bless that lady, whoever she is—and told her my daughter couldn't breathe," said Abby. She then would then watch helplessly in the hallway as a team of doctors, nurses, and respiratory therapists took over. Abby said, "Anybody you can imagine came and helped out and brought her back to life, because at that point she didn't have oxygen. We knew whatever had happened to her had progressed so far that her lungs were not working anymore. So she was intubated and completely sedated. She was a quadriplegic, and she was on a respirator. That was the lowest point."

According to Julie Connelly, a respiratory therapist, Leah could no longer move her diaphragm, the muscles that control movement of the lungs. They were shutting down as the paralysis was progressing. Julie explained how the procedure to intubate involved moving the tongue out of the way and inserting a breathing tube between her vocal cords.

Julie had arrived at the hospital that morning just before seven o'clock to begin her shift in the pediatric intensive care unit (PICU) when a therapist came up from the ER looking for a device that measures the depth of a breath. "I had a sense it wasn't good," said Julie, who brought the device with her to the ER and became part of the team that would work on Leah.

"From the tests they asked me to perform, she was not able to generate anything. I knew right off the bat this was serious. It was only a matter of time before Leah probably would have stopped breathing completely. She was working really, really hard, like her whole body was lifting as she was trying to get some air. That's when we intubated her and put her on the ventilator."

Abby was aware of the severity of the situation, that Leah's life was now in the balance. She carefully texted Peter. "I thought, *I can't call to say, 'I'm afraid Leah is going to die, and you have to come to the hospital right away,'* because how can you tell someone to drive ten miles after hearing that news? So I just texted him, 'You might want to hurry up; please come to the hospital.'"

Peter got there as quickly as he could and saw Leah. "She certainly wasn't the girl we knew twenty-four hours ago. She wasn't even the girl I said goodbye to a few hours ago," he remembered.

"She's completely sedated; she's unconscious. She's got tubes in her nose, tubes in her arms. I came back [to the Morristown hospital], and it's as if she's gone. In twenty-four hours, she went from playing softball and running around to being quadriplegic. You saw everything you thought you'd do with your kids—the vacations, the sports, everything a normal family thinks of—is gone."

Dr. Beth Singer, the Hansen family's pediatrician, explained how fortunate it was that Leah was not on the floor upstairs in the PICU but in the ER, with her mother at her side, to alert nurses when she could no longer breathe. This proximity allowed her to be surrounded by a team of emergency room professionals hastily put together. Time mattered. Had there been a delay of even a few minutes, and she lacked oxygen for a significant period, she would have suffered brain damage. "When you're on the floor [in the PICU], you're not getting people as experienced as the people in the emergency room," said Dr. Singer.

That Tuesday night, Leah had an MRI that took nearly three hours, with inconclusive results. Abby and Peter were told by Dr. Singer that Leah was affected by rare and unique symptoms. "Dr. Singer reinforced that Leah's a 'tough kid' and 'we'll figure this out,'" Abby explained in a text message to family and friends. "We can do this. I know God loves His daughter Leah more than I do, which seems incomprehensible. She's trying so hard to move her little limbs. Pray for a miracle."

"In a dark conference room in full tears, we asked God 'for a lame little girl to walk.' We humbly ask you to do the same," wrote Peter in a text message to the family He later measured the moment as "rock bottom."

"We have the God of the universe, who knows every cell in Leah's body, working on it," Leah's aunt Carrie wrote in a text on the family's message board.

In the first few days, the doctors remained puzzled. "She doesn't have oddball diseases. She doesn't have an infection. She doesn't have meningitis," said Peter, recalling what the doctors had told him. "One of the things they threw out early on was that she could have had a stroke of her spinal cord. But, no, she probably didn't have that because it is so rare. If it's not that, it's something else, but it's hard to know what's going on."

Then came the positive sign on the third day when Leah was asked to move her toes. She had the faintest wiggle in her right toes. Abby and Peter wanted to shout this from the rooftop of the hospital, *Leah wiggled her right toe!*

"We sent that [message] out to everybody who was praying for her, as a celebration. In our minds, we took that as a message from God: 'Don't worry, I have this. It's been three days, and you've been patient, and I'm going to give you a sign.' The farthest thing from the center of her body is the toe, and she moved her toes," said Abby.

This was our olive branch. Noah learned it was the beginning of the end of the Flood when the dove sent from the ark returned with a small olive branch. The floodwaters were receding. Leah could move her right toes! It wasn't lost on us that it was on the *third day*.

Often during the first few days, fluid would build in her lungs, and her oxygen level would plummet. Peter or Abby would hurry from the room in the PICU and summon help, and the fluids would be suctioned. I appreciate how Abby did not kick us out of the room during this process, to understand the severity. It was another rock bottom, in the trenches.

The earliest signs that Leah's brain was not affected by a loss of oxygen that first morning in the ER was when the television in her room was on and one of the characters in a bubble-gum sitcom said a word that is prohibited in the Hansen house. By the expression on Leah's face, it was apparent that she feared maybe Mom and Dad would no longer let her watch a show that used forbidden language. "There was great relief in that. Her mind is still there. Throughout the whole time, God gave us little glimpses that He was in control," said Peter.

On Friday, there was another small victory. A friend had dropped off a joke book, and Abby and Leah selected one joke to be the joke they would tell the doctors and nurses. When Peter came into the room, Abby tried out the joke, but she botched the punchline. Leah came to her mother's rescue. "And though she struggled to mouth the words around the breathing tube, she corrected me. That's my Leah! She will be back!"

Later that day, she bent her right leg at the knee and kicked a pillow off the bed. "As for Abby and me, the outpouring of prayer, love, and support is overwhelming. The hardest challenges of our life are bringing the greatest blessings," Peter texted.

Donna remembered seeing Leah the first day she was no longer sedated. "Leah was Leah. Those eyes, beautiful blue eyes looking above the tubes, arms that couldn't move. But there were those eyes. She tried to mouth, 'Hello, Nana,' around the tubes. Nana was trying not to dissolve in tears."

Abby and Peter made it known to visitors there was one absolute rule: no crying in Leah's hospital room! "Act silly, act ridiculous, but one tear, and you must take a hike," Donna recalled.

During one early visit, Donna was about to enter the room when she met Julie Bearchell, who was leaving the room. Julie, one of Abby's roommates at Messiah College, had flown up from Atlanta to visit Abby and Leah and was leaving the room when she and Donna met. "Together we just collapsed in tears. No need to talk. It was time for weeping in the hallway," said Donna. She then wiped away her tears and entered Leah's room.

"The first time we visited, seeing Leah hooked up to so many machines, lying there paralyzed, was both terrifying and heartbreaking," said Peter's mother Ann. "At first, I was numb. In the days to come, we continued to visit, but seeing Leah on a respirator pressed down on me the most."

On Saturday, Abby wrote to the mothers of the girls who were to be at Leah's sleepover birthday party, scheduled for the following Friday. She explained the physical challenges and told the moms, "Most importantly 'she's' still there. Although she cannot speak when I speak of your daughters, she smiles and remembers. When I tell stories or refer to things we've done or plan to do so, she responds just as she should. Her brain is intact. As her group of closest friends, I'm pleading for your prayers. Come, Lord Jesus."

Tim Lucas, the senior pastor of Liquid Church, where Abby and Peter met during its founding years, had come within the first twenty-four hours and he told Abby and Peter how Jesus healed the lame for a reason. "It was to show *His* glory and point people to *Him*. This miracle will do the same."

Lucas remembered a story from the Gospel of Mark that he learned as a kid in Sunday school and later preached sermons on. It was about how Jesus went to the house of Jairus, a synagogue ruler whose fourteen-year-old daughter had died. Mark wrote, "[Jesus] went in where the child was. He took her by the hand and said to her *Talitha Koum* (which means, 'Little girl, I say to you, get up!'). She stood right up and walked" (Mark 5:41).

Talitha Koum. That saying in Aramaic became our battle cry.

"We are one day closer to the miracle. I can't wait to tell the story. It's going to change lives for eternity," our daughter Carrie texted that Saturday.

On Sunday of the next week, a score of visitors came. A friend who teaches music brought her ukulele and sang Girl Scout, Sunday school, and Taylor Swift songs. Abby's cousin, Emily Gritters, painted Leah's fingernails a glittery pink. Two softball coaches came, and Leah showed off her right leg by kicking a softball off the bed. The no-tear-zone hospital room was decorated with stuffed animals and posters. Leah remembered, "It snowed a lot that week. I guess my friends had nothing better to do than make a poster for Leah."

Among the treasured pictures of Leah was one taken by a professional photographer the previous spring. Abby asked Leah's Aunt Sarah to make a copy Abby could put in the room, so that hospital staff could see their patient at her very best.

Still, on the seventh day, there was no diagnosis.

On the ninth day in the PICU, a Wednesday, Abby participated in a meeting with the doctors and nurses working Leah's case. She texted to the family, "Apparently in the 'whole hospital' her case is the #1 priority. They are calling docs from other states today and soliciting opinions. However, it's no coincidence that our church is having a service of worship and *healing* tonight. She will *rise*, and we will give *Him* all the praise."

That night, Liquid Church held the prayer service at the church's main campus in Parsippany, a service that had been scheduled months earlier. Peter and members of our family were there as the staff laid hands on him and prayed for Leah. Meanwhile, as prayers were sent from Parsippany, Leah was being prepared for a second MRI. The first MRI had not been easy. Abby and Leah dreaded a second one. The second one would be even worse.

"It did not go well," said Abby. "We were having temperature control issues with the room. She was to be partially sedated, but the sedative was not strong enough. So they called me and said, 'Mom, do you want to come in here? She seems upset.' She was crying and crying and still breathing aided by a breathing tube. 'When will this be over? When will this be over?' And I told the doctors, 'I am staying here for the rest of the procedure.' She was in the MRI tube, and I was hugging around her knees, as close as I could get so she would know I was there.

"I prayed as she's crying, 'This will not be wasted. This will not be wasted.' I knew whatever happened that night was going to be big. This will not be wasted. The experience for her, the experience for us, was so horrible. We didn't want it to be wasted.

"I said to one of them [in the room where the MRI was happening], 'I don't know what Leah's story is going to be, but she will be healed.' That's all I want people to remember. As strange as her affliction was, she would be healed by Jesus."

On the tenth day of Leah's hospitalization, Abby received the ultimate diagnosis when Donna and her sister Amy Fiorilla were visiting. Dr. Harvey Bennett, the neurologist in charge of Leah's care, asked Abby to come alone into the conference room. With tears in his eyes, he told Abby that Leah had suffered a spinal cord stroke. Abby recalled that Aunt Amy brought her homemade soup. She figures she threw the soup down the drain. She had no stomach for anything. None of us did.

We would learn that fewer than 2 percent of strokes are spinal cord strokes, when vessels feeding blood to the spinal cord are blocked. Most strokes affect the brain. Of the ones that affect the spinal cord, only a tiny fraction of them occur in healthy eight-year-old girls.

Though the doctors call it a spinal cord stroke, a more correct technical term would be a spinal cord infarction. Strokes in the brain occur when blood clots form inside a vessel. What likely happened with Leah is that a foreign body—perhaps a bone chip or gelatinous material from her spinal cord—was inside the vessel, cutting the oxygen supply to a section of her spinal cord.

With the diagnosis, Abby and Peter considered the consequences. They feared Leah would be confined to a wheelchair. I remember thinking how Peter had built up so much goodwill with men in the church and in the community, there would be no shortage of volunteers to help him make renovations to the house to accommodate a handicapped girl. Peter was thinking how he would have to upgrade the family van.

On the eleventh day, Leah used an iPad, and with help from Mom and Dad, she tapped a message, "Yay it is my birthday!" She asked Abby if she would be home for her party, scheduled for a few days away.

"I explained that I told all the mommies we'll have the party later when we feel our best and we can plan. She was totally OK with that! Phew!"

On March 19, she began the process of regulating her own

breathing with a CPAP device that would replace the ventilator. The goal was to breathe on her own for a half hour. With respiratory therapist Julie Connelly monitoring the test, Leah regulated her breathing for thirty-five minutes. "She did great. A-plus," said Julie. It was good enough for her to be taken off the ventilator.

"The tube is out! Everything is great," Peter reported on the family message board. Leah's throat was parched and talking would be a challenge.

The following day, Leah spoke into a camera with a whispery, "Thank you for praying." The video would be played at the Liquid Church campuses that Sunday.

"Hearing your voice is such a gift," her aunt Elizabeth Jemison texted from South Carolina.

The next morning when I entered her room, she said, "Hello, Baba."

Another challenge at the Morristown hospital had been to wean Leah from a process called desaturation, in which a tube was inserted into her throat to suck fluid from her lung. On Sunday, March 24, Peter went to the Liquid Church campus in Somerville, where he and Jon Coords, the campus pastor, prayed before the early service. "We were begging God to do a miracle," said Peter.

Hours earlier, around four in the morning, Leah had to be desaturated again. If the problem persisted, it was possible that a tracheostomy would be required. Peter and Jon were praying for a miracle, not knowing that five hours earlier, Leah had had fluid suctioned from her lungs for the last time. Their prayer had been answered that morning.

With her breathing stabilized, plans were made to transfer Leah to Children's Specialized Hospital in New Brunswick to begin physical therapy. Peter had spoken with a family friend who practiced medicine in the Washington, DC, area, and the friend contacted a doctor at Children's Hospital of Philadelphia (CHOP), regularly ranked as one of the best in the world.

The doctor at CHOP told Peter that Leah indeed could be transferred to Philadelphia, though it would require transport by helicopter. The doctor then reassured Peter and Abby that the hospital in New Brunswick was excellent, giving Peter and Abby confidence it would be the right place. Peter said he did not want the stress of a helicopter ride, and the hospital in New Brunswick would be more convenient than Philadelphia for the extended family and friends to visit.

As Leah was being prepared to leave the Morristown hospital, Julie Connelly paid one last visit to her room. Though she was not working in the PICU that week, she helped Leah one more time with her therapy and then prepared her and Abby for the forty-five-minute trip to New Brunswick in an ambulance.

In conversations with Julie, Abby and Peter had learned that she was the friend of a friend of Peter's and was a committed Christian. When Abby meets a Christian, she tells Leah and the other kids, "This person loves Jesus just as much as we do."

"I know [Abby and Peter] are praying people, praying for a miracle. I understood their faith and what Abby was asking of God. I understood how scared Abby was. She was so strong, but she was terrified inside. As I would be," said Julie.

Julie said Abby could have sent Leah to bed that Monday night when her body went limp, with plans to take her to the doctor in the morning if she did not get better. Leah would have stopped breathing when she was sleeping. "Honestly, she would not have made it. God's hand was on Abby and Leah. God was protecting you guys," Julie told me.

Julie recalled the day the breathing tube was removed.

"Leah was very nervous, very anxious. She was scared. The fear of a tube coming out, you can't breathe—that's real. But she trusted me and was happy when I was there."

Julie kept up with the story of Leah as Abby reported small victories on Facebook, such as the time Leah was able to pick up a Goldfish snack with her right hand. The next year, she watched Facebook videos of Leah skiing down the bunny slope and playing softball and field hockey with limited use of her arms.

By the spring of 2020, Leah was once again riding a bike, using muscle memory from before the spinal cord stroke. As Peter and I rode with her on the streets of Ocean Grove, we recognized how it might have been nearly impossible to teach her to ride a bike without that old memory.

In February 2021, three years after the spinal cord stroke, Donna and I and Leah and her family spent Presidents' Day weekend in Upstate New York, where Peter's family has a cabin on the opposite side of Lake Pleasant from Camp of the Woods, a Christian conference center. One month earlier, Leah had fallen on the ski slope and suffered a hairline fracture of her right arm, her good arm. She did not want to take it easy. "Google says four to six weeks [recovery]," Leah reported to us.

Now it was four weeks after breaking her good arm, and Leah was going to try to parallel ski. There would be no more forming a pizza slice with the tips of the skis. "I'm terrified," she told her mom. But by the end of the day, she was parallel skiing. Also that weekend, she was tooling around on a snowmobile, with her right arm doing the steering. She refused to be babied. On March 5, 2022, the fourth anniversary of her stroke, she skied at Gore Mountain in Upstate New York.

Abby and Peter, said Julie, "are not afraid to let her be a kid. All of these things are helping her get stronger, giving her joy.

If you kept her home in a bubble, and the other kids could go out and play and she couldn't, she'd be so sad.

"It builds my faith. I love to see God at work. The Lord knew I would be doing this, and I would be there the day she came in. Maybe God picked me to help Leah get through her worst day. Just to be part of the journey, just a small part, seeing her smile, makes me grateful for what I do. God can use me as a respiratory therapist. It's nice to be in the middle of the story."

As Leah was about to leave the Morristown hospital, Abby removed the scores of cards, posters, stuffed animals, and softball jerseys that had decorated her room in the PICU. Owing to her popularity at church and in the community, as many as twenty-three people had visited that room in a single day.

On March 30, 2018, Leah was wheeled out of the PICU to a waiting ambulance to take them to the Children's Specialized Hospital, where mother and daughter would spend the next two months. The day before she was discharged from Morristown, her feeding tube and IV were removed. No more masking tape on her face. Abby and Leah rode in the ambulance to what Abby called "the gymnastics hospital." When Abby texted a picture of Leah riding in the ambulance, Donna texted that the hospital should be alerted: "New Brunswick, watch out. A multitude of angels are coming!"

"This place [in Morristown] is for sick people. Soon that will not be her," Abby wrote. After bittersweet goodbyes to the Morristown staff who had come to adore Leah and bond with Abby, she was wheeled out of the hospital on March 30.

It had been Peter's prayer that Leah would *walk* out of the Morristown hospital. That prayer would be answered later. On Christmas Eve. Keep reading.

Joseph, Timothy, Leah, and Serena Hansen, Fall 2016

Leah, Spring 2017

The Long Hill Twisters Softball Team, Summer 2017

Leah playing softball in Long Hill, Spring 2017

CHAPTER 2

A New Girl

I t was our prayer that Leah would be treated in the ER on
that first Monday and be healed immediately, like that story
in the fifth chapter of Mark when Jesus *immediately* healed the
daughter of the synagogue ruler. It was not to be. She had spent
more than three weeks in Morristown before arriving in New
Brunswick on Good Friday.

On that first Good Friday, when the Son of God was on
the cross, he said to the Father, "My God, My God, why have
You forsaken me?" repeating words of David from Psalm 22.
Commenting on that psalm, English preacher Charles Haddon
Spurgeon (1834–1892) wrote, "If prayer be unanswered, it is
not because God is unfaithful, but for some good and weighty
reason."

Two thousand years ago, there was a good and weighty
reason for Jesus to remain on the cross and die a horrible death.
"He who knew no sin became sin for us, so that in Him we
might become the righteousness of God" (2 Corinthians 5:21).
On the third day, Jesus would rise from the dead, on what
Christians celebrate as Easter Sunday.

What if our prayers had been answered *immediately?* Leah
might have spent that Monday night in the hospital with a

bad case of the flu and perhaps been discharged the next day. Because of a rare March blizzard, school was closed for the rest of the week. Had she been healed immediately, Leah would have returned to school the following Monday with a story about her one night in the hospital, and who would have been interested? Our family would have remembered the time Leah went to the ER, just like we remember the time her brother Timmy went to the ER to get stitches. In again, out again. (And there would be no book.) That would have been our forty-eight-hour script. But God had a different plan.

Two days after she was admitted to the children's rehabilitation hospital, on Easter Sunday, our extended family joined Peter, Abby, and Leah in the hospital's community room. For the first time in nearly a month, Timmy, Serena, and Joey got to see their older sister and their mommy.

The following day, Leah was fitted for a motorized wheelchair. "All I kept thinking is this would be the most perfect job for Timmy. You have to measure, build, modify," Abby reported.

Leah also had a roommate, a thirteen-year-old girl who was recovering from an infection to her spinal cord. Her new roomie asked Leah if she wanted to play a board game in the rec room. "I mean, a thirteen-year-old girl is basically Leah's dream anyway," said Aunt Carrie.

The thought of rehab beginning the day after Easter made Leah nervous. But she would come to love it, and the following morning, Abby let her sleep until 9:45 a.m. "I had to fend off pesky people looking for blood pressure, to give medications, to check this or that. Doesn't everybody know sleep is the best medicine?" wrote Abby.

That Friday, one month after her stroke, Leah slept without needing a breathing mask, and her oxygen level was 100 percent.

A nurse who had not seen Leah for several days said, "Leah, you look like a new girl. Do you feel any different?"

"I feel like I did before I got sick," she said.

When Donna read Abby's text, she said she was crying happy tears. Abby responded, "Oh, Leah's used to those tears. [She says,] 'Mommy cries every day.' Leah always rolls her eyes and smiles."

Two weeks after they arrived in New Brunswick, Abby said she had not cried in a week, despite what Leah reported. "And then a nurse named Shannon came into our room," Abby said.

In the first few days, Shannon Silverstein had seen Leah in her wheelchair on the hospital floor, and one day she was assigned to her. She learned from her chart that Leah had suffered a spinal cord stroke. "My first impression was that she had a real good attitude. We didn't do much that day. Her mom preferred to do things herself. The only time they needed me was when I brought her medicine in the morning."

Shannon regularly listened to Tim Lucas's online sermons, produced by Liquid Church. While making dinner one night, she listened to his Easter sermon, and Pastor Tim was talking about a girl who the church was praying for. "He didn't say her name yet. He said she had had a stroke, and I said, 'My goodness, that sounds like the patient I had.' Then he said her name. Leah Hansen. I was floored. I was brought to tears when he spoke the scripture, 'Little girl, I say to you, get up and walk.'"

The next day, Shannon told Abby about hearing the sermon. "She loved hearing [Leah's] backstory," said Abby. "She said she prays every day for all the patients and all the parents. She reminded me that we serve a God of miracles, and she believes in the power of prayer. Of course, by this time, we are both crying buckets. What an encouragement, that she would follow

God's lead and work so hard and pray for all these kids as well. Jesus is just everywhere in this journey."

"These angels just keep popping up," Donna texted the family.

What impressed Shannon was Abby and Peter's devotion to their child, with Abby sharing the room in the hospital day and night, supported by a constant flow of family and friends. Shannon explained that having a positive outlook can have a role in the healing process. "Their attitude can change the output. When we put our hope in God and do everything we need to do, then the power of prayer can lift us."

Two weeks later, Shannon attended a church leadership conference in Birmingham, Alabama, and it turned out Tim Lucas was there too. She introduced herself and told him she was a nurse for "Little Leah Hansen." They recorded a video together and sent it to Abby.

The morning that Shannon introduced herself to Abby, our son Andrew and his wife, Elizabeth, had prayed at their home in South Carolina. Elizabeth wrote, "We prayed for Leah's therapy today and for an extra dose of encouragement." Shannon was the extra dose.

On April 18, Leah achieved another milestone when, with the help of a therapist, she stood in the rec room, balancing on her own. "Muscles! Muscles!" implored the therapist as she held Leah's thighs before letting go.

Timmy watched the video three times and said, "Hallelujah, she can stand."

Leah said to Abby and the therapist, "I can finally move on with my life, people!"

On April 20, three members of the Rutgers gymnastics team came to Leah's room. The girls raised their fists for Leah's

"Strong Like a Girl" pose. Later, members of Rutgers' football, softball, soccer, volleyball, and women's track teams visited.

The next day, Peter posted a video of Leah finally moving her left foot, seven weeks after the stroke. Strokes in the brain often affect one side of the body more than the other. Leah's right side is her dominant side, while her left side remains most affected by the stroke. Andrew and Elizabeth went out to dinner that night, after seeing the video, Elizabeth's loud prayers in the South Carolina restaurant drew odd stares, when she prayed, "Thank you, God, for the left foot!"

Several days later, Leah achieved a major achievement, a Neil Armstrong walking-on-the-moon milestone. Abby planned to go to dinner that night in downtown New Brunswick with Donna and Carrie, who would be celebrating her birthday the next day. Peter's sister, Sarah Hansen, came to the hospital to stay with Leah, who had a bold plan. She wanted to walk across the room, about five feet from her bed to the bed Abby slept in. Leah recalled that when Carrie entered the room, she said to her, "'I have a surprise for you,' and I walked from my bed to Mom's couch-bed situation."

Sarah remembered, "Abby helped her stand and then let go. In that moment, I saw prayers being answered and felt the presence of the Lord. That first step, that first bend of the knee, that first sign of assurance: He was with us. Leah turned around and returned to her own bed."

In the next few days, she went to the rooftop garden at the hospital and planted flowers, and she went to the kitchen and baked cookies. Soon she was able to walk to her classes in the hospital, where a tutor helped her with her homework.

On May 8, Abby and Leah talked about going home and playing "hospital" with her friends, using Leah's wheelchair. "I've got news for you, honey," said her therapist. "I'm not sending you home with a wheelchair." Doorways in the house in Long Hill would not have to be widened. One of the blessings was that the stroke did not affect the portion of her spinal cord that controlled movement of her legs the way it affected her arms. Otherwise, Leah likely would likely have needed a wheelchair for the rest of her life.

On May 9, the children's hospital hosted a prom for the kids. In preparation for the event, Leah went on her first field trip in a hospital van, going to Target to pick out a prom dress. When the teal and white dress she favored turned out to be too short, Carrie ordered the correct size online. The day of the prom, a beautician applied makeup to Leah, a manicurist did her nails, and Abby removed tangles from Leah's long blond hair. She marched into the prom and danced the night away as best she could. She was the belle of the ball. One hospital employee said all the effort to prepare a prom for all the children—the band, the buffet, the photographer—was worth it just to see Leah Hansen dance.

Leah was discharged on May 31, signing her own out-of-the-building pass and stepping into her dad's van wearing a sling on her left arm and brace on her left leg. The rest of us left with fond memories of what Leah had become. Each time visitors entered the building, they passed *The Magic Fountain*, a sculpture by J. Seward Johnson, depicting kids dancing under sprays of water, with an explanation, "The design captures each child as they enter the fountain's water transforming the children from their realistic form into shiny silver ... meaning they are healed." The hospital's mission: "To welcome and encourage patients and their families." It was a pause-for-pictures day for Leah and the rest of us.

Unlike her trip in Abby's van to the ER in Morristown, this

time Leah wore a seat belt. She slept in her own bed, and her mom let her sleep until nine in the morning.

On June 3, she was welcomed back to Liquid Church, greeted with a banner and balloons. The next day, she returned to her third-grade class at Millington School to a similar greeting. Throughout the day, Jennifer Dawson, the principal, and Noelle Milito, Leah's third-grade teacher, sent Abby a stream of pictures of Leah.

Leah had developed a relationship with the hospital staff, who turned her into their cover girl. As part of fundraising campaigns for the hospital and the Children's Miracle Network, her image has appeared on posters at Walmart, Costco, and Wawa and Speedway convenience stores. She participated in events hosted by IHOP. She represented New Jersey at an event Speedway hosted in Dayton, Ohio.

In June 2021 Leah spoke at a fundraising golf tournament at Fiddler's Elbow Country Club in Bedminster, benefiting the Children's Specialized Hospital.

At the breakfast that preceded the golf event, Leah spoke to about 150 people, mostly men. "She held the audience in the palm of her hand. There wasn't a sound in the room," said Philip Salerno, the president and chief development officer for the Children's Specialized Hospital Foundation. "I could not believe how she is so poised speaking in public. What was she, twelve years old? Amazing."

Leah had spoken at earlier events and, she said, "I winged it. That's what Mom always did." But for this event, she explained, "I wrote bullet points on a napkin. I wanted to leave out the ums and pauses, and I told a few jokes."

Four years earlier, she was in a hospital bed, communicating by blinking her eyes when Mom or Dad pointed to the right letter. Now she was a confident twelve-year-old, using bullet points to address a room of 150.

She explained to the crowd how she especially liked therapy in the swimming pool. "When I said, 'What nine-year-old girl doesn't like a pool?' the people laughed."

CHAPTER 3

Christmas Miracle

The year of our Lord 2018 was not yet over when Leah had a setback in December and had to be readmitted with breathing problems to the PICU at the Morristown Medical Center.

"I was nearly broken," Abby posted on Facebook. "This roadblock in her recovery that had gone so well was just devastating. Could a nine-year-old spend her birthday, Easter AND Christmas in the hospital? Could her Mom keep up the smiles? It seems that the hills and valleys of 2018 will keep it interesting until the very end."

With her lungs still weak, Leah could not shake the effects of the common cold and was hospitalized with pneumonia and respiratory syncytial virus (RSV). That night, Donna and I were in New York City, attending a performance of *The Messiah* at Carnegie Hall, but our hearts and minds were in Morristown. As we sat in the second row in the second tier, others in our section had to be appalled by our behavior. *Those guys are on their cell phones! At Carnegie Hall? During The Messiah?* When the "Hallelujah Chorus" was being sung, Donna was listening from the lobby, while on the phone with Abby.

Leah's battalion of prayer warriors responded to the

latest hospitalization. "Your daughter is a fighter, and she will continue to tackle the next obstacle. Have a good night and continue to be held in God's arms," wrote Jennifer Dawson, the Millington School principal. On December 21, the last day of school before Christmas break, Leah was able to do FaceTime with her third-grade classmates.

On December 22, Abby reported, "The x-ray was just awful." A healthy x-ray would have revealed two dark lungs. Leah's left lung was a milky white. She was breathing with only one healthy lung, and Christmas was three days away. Our family agreed that Christmas morning might have to wait, that our calendars would be frozen until Leah was discharged.

On Christmas Eve, at 4:00 a.m., Leah wrote on her whiteboard: "Can you get me out of here for Christmas?"

Dr. Erin Johnson, her primary physician, smiled at her young patient's request. The x-ray that morning, according to Dr. Johnson, "looks fantastically amazing. We are all on Team Leah to make a miracle happen and get you home for Christmas."

"I didn't know if this was going to happen," said Abby. "But if I have to, I will be strapping oxygen on my back, and I'm taking her home."

Julie Connelly, the respiratory therapist who helped Leah regain her breath back in March, was working that week at the Morristown Medical Center. Under normal conditions, Julie recalled, "Leah probably would have stayed one more night. But it was Christmas Eve. I told the doctors she would be fine. She needed to get out of bed and walk. I gave [the doctors] my vote of confidence. You know a little miracle occurred there."

A boatload of medical equipment would be delivered to the house in Long Hill, and Julie gave Abby and Peter a crash course of instructions. "I got to spend a lot of time with them, with a ton of equipment delivered in my presence. I taught them how to use it. I wanted to make sure they were confident. It was good to see her. I had never really heard her voice. When she left in March, her voice was weak, almost whispering. Now I was able to hear her speak with a strong voice. 'Oh, this is what you sound like.'"

That afternoon, the prayer that Peter prayed nine months ago in March was answered, and it was not lost on any of us. Leah would *walk* out of the Morristown hospital. He sent us a video of her pressing the button that opened the exit doors in the PICU. She would wake up on Christmas morning in her own bed.

That was the year 2018. From those first alarming text messages on March 5 through Christmas morning, Leah was the focus of our energy, our plans, and our prayers.

But in God's economy, that is the story with all of us. The God who can name the stars, mind the sparrows, and count the hairs on your head knows who you are and exactly what you are thinking. Yes, you.

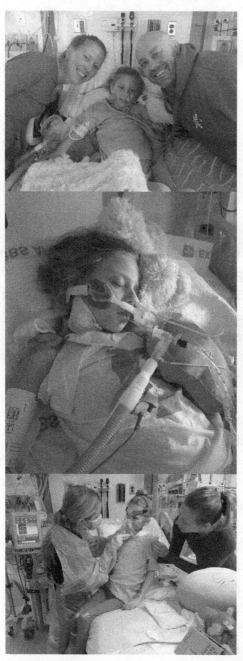

Leah in the Morristown Memorial Hospital Pediatric ICU, March, 2018

CHAPTER 4

"Thou Are Mine"

If I could slip a verse into the Bible, it would be the words of English poet and hymn writer Henry Kirke White: "God, without question, beholds as distinctly the actions of every man, as if that man were the only created being, and the Godhead were solely employed in observing him."

Actually, I did add that to my own Bible, when I enlarged the type, copied it, and pasted in the inside cover, as a reminder that God knows me and Leah and my readers the way he knew Henry Kirke White, who was weakened by tuberculosis, writing this before dying in 1806 at the age of twenty-one.

There is a popular tourist site in Paris, the resting place of the skeletal remains of seven million souls. The Paris Catacombs are located five stories beneath the city streets—131 steps down and 112 steps up to the gift shop. Visitors are cautioned: "Arrête, c'est ici l'empire de la mort!" (Stop! This is the empire of death!)

Once at the bottom, you can walk nearly a metric mile past a neat row of skulls and bones in tunnels that had been mined centuries ago for limestone to construct many of the city's landmark buildings. The skulls are arranged in careful patterns. "They encourage visitors toward introspection and a meditation on death," according to the website posted by Les Catacombes de Paris.

I remember staring at one random skull, three rows from the floor, and thinking about something we impressed on young reporters at the newspaper: Everyone has a story. On closest inspection, no two of the seven million skulls will be alike, and each of the millions of souls died with a unique story.

I wanted to ask my chosen skull, *Mon ami. what is your story? Tell me about the life you lived. Your family. Your challenges. And while I have you here, what did you think of Gustave Eiffel's idea for a tower?* (Actually, Gustave Eiffel began building the tower in 1887, while the last skull had been placed in the Catacombs in 1860, the year of Lincoln's first inauguration.)

The God of the Bible knew all seven million stories. He also knew the story of everyone who would share space with us in a crowded car on the Paris subway later that night, and at that very moment every soul at the Mall of America, on the Rome, London, and New York subways, and every one of the 111,441 spectators my son Andrew and I sat with at a football game we attended The Big House on the University of Michigan campus.

There is a story in the fifth chapter of the Gospel of Mark, several verses before the *Talitha Koum* story. On his way to the home of the synagogue ruler whose daughter was dying, Jesus was pressed by a crowd. A woman tugged on his garment. What was her story, and how did Jesus even feel the random tug? Her story was that she suffered for twelve years from bleeding that would not stop. She had gone to countless physicians, and none could heal her. According to Jewish law, she was unclean.

Jesus stopped and asked his followers a question they must have thought absurd. "Who touched my clothes?" It was probably not unlike a crowded subway. The woman in the crush came forward, trembling with fear, saying it was her.

"Daughter," said Jesus, "your faith has healed you. Go in peace and be freed from your suffering" (Mark 5:14).

At that one moment in time, Jesus of Nazareth, the second member of the Trinity, was focused on one person among scores on a crowded street. If God can keep His eye on a sparrow, then surely He knew Leah Hansen's story, from eternity past, in ways we cannot understand.

For eighty-seven days in two hospitals, Leah had doctors, nurses, and therapists focused on children like her. She had Abby and Peter and an extended family whose lives were concentrated on her. Friends were thinking about and praying for her. Altogether, she had an amazing support team. But in God's economy, Leah is no different from the rest of us. We all have, according to Henry Kirke White, the Godhead paying attention.

"If I could hear Christ praying for me in the next room, I would not fear a million enemies. Yet distance makes no difference. He is praying for me," wrote Robert Murray M'Cheyne (1813–1843), a preacher with the Church of Scotland.

In her novel *Uncle Tom's Cabin*, Harriet Beecher Stowe tells the story of Tom, who had been sold into slavery to the evil Simon Legree. When Legree apprehended Tom, he rifled through Tom's pocket, taking his silk handkerchief and a few small trinkets that Tom treasured. With a "contemptuous grunt," he tossed the trinkets in the river. Simon Legree then discovered Tom's small Methodist hymnbook.

Stowe wrote: "Humph! Pious to be sure. So what's yer name—you belong to the church, eh?

"Yes Mas'r," said Tom firmly.

"Well, I'll soon have that out of you. I'll have none o' yer bawling, praying, singing [Negroes] in my place … *I'm* your church now! You understand—you've got to do as *I* say."

Stowe continued: "Something within the silent black man

answered *No!* And, as if repeated by an invisible voice, came the words of an old prophetic scroll. As Eva [daughter of the plantation owner] had often read [from the Old Testament book of Isaiah] to Tom: 'Fear not! For I have redeemed thee. I have called thee by name. Thou art *mine!*'"

Uncle Tom? "Mine."

The woman bleeding for twelve years? "Mine."

Leah Hansen? "Mine."

Tacked on the bulletin board in Leah's room at the Morristown hospital was a message written on lined paper by seven-year-old Matthew Gill, "I have called you by name you are mine Ishaih 43:1. Love Matthew."

When an airplane is in distress and the pilot communicates with ground control, ground control will want to know how many people are on board. The pilot will not say, "We have sixty-three passengers, five crew members, the copilot and myself." Instead, the pilot will say, "We have seventy souls on board." Ground control will then prepare for seventy souls to rescue. In the economy of the moment, the soul of the pilot is as important as the soul of the obscure passenger cowering in seat 14D.

C. S. Lewis wrote in *The Problem of Pain*, "The signature on each soul may be a product of heredity and environment, but that only means that heredity and environment are among the instruments whereby God creates a soul. I am considering not how, but why, He makes each soul unique. If He had no use for all these differences, I do not see why He should have created more souls than one."

Lewis added: "But God will look to every soul like its first love because He is its first love. Your place in heaven will seem to be made for you and you alone, because you were made for it—made for it like stitch by stitch is made for a glove."

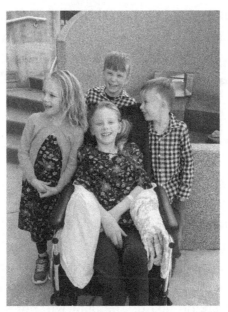

*Leah and her siblings on Easter Sunday at
Children's Specialized Hospital, 2018*

Leah inpatient at Children's Specialized Hospital, Spring 2018

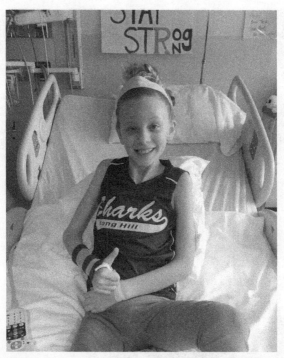

Leah wearing her team jersey on Little League Opening Day, Spring 2018

Maggie Caputo visiting Leah at Children's
Specialized Hospital, Spring 2018

Grace Eline visiting Leah at Children's Specialized Hospital, Spring 2018

Discharge Day- heading home on May 31, 2018

*Family photo at Children's Specialized Hospital
on discharge day, May 31, 2018*

CHAPTER 5

Dark Seasons

Former Major League Baseball pitcher Jim Kaat was part of a broadcast team for a New York Yankees game when a low-scoring pitchers' duel was expected. Instead, both teams scored in bunches. A high-scoring slugfest, as they say. Said Kaat, "You can't script baseball."

Boxer Mike Tyson put it even better: "Everyone has a plan 'til they get punched in the mouth."

We were punched in the mouth when Leah suddenly got sick; when my youngest sister, Ginny, was diagnosed with a cancer that led to her painful death; when Donna's mother had a stroke and later was killed in a car accident; when Donna's sister, Joyce Johnson, was killed by a drunk driver. How could a God who calls all of us "Mine" allow these things to happen?

Christians are left to ponder: If God is all-powerful and if God is all-loving, why does He permit His children to suffer? Why did God not intervene when the body of an eight-year-old girl was gradually shutting down? Where was God when my cousin's seventeen-year-old granddaughter died suddenly on a high school soccer field? Why did six million Jews die in the Holocaust?

"The fact of suffering undoubtedly constitutes the single

greatest challenge to the Christian faith and has been in every generation," wrote John R.W. Stott.

"Dark seasons are part of the journey," said Tim Lucas, the lead pastor of Liquid Church, during a series of sermons from the Old Testament book of Habakkuk.

Remarkably, the apostle Paul refers to the "joy of suffering." Joy? Seriously? Understand this was a man who was beaten, flogged, whipped, and shipwrecked. "I have been in danger from rivers, in danger from bandits, in danger from my own countrymen, in danger from Gentiles, in danger in the city, in danger in the country, in danger at sea, in danger from false brothers" (2 Corinthians 11:26). He knew hunger, thirst, and nakedness. He did some of his most significant writing while in prison, never once complaining in his letters about the lousy prison food. All he ever asked for was a winter coat.

"Don't look forward to the day you stop suffering, because when it comes, you'll know you're dead," playwright Tennessee Williams told the *Observer* of London.

"It is true that I have had heartache and tragedy in my life. These are things none of us avoids. Suffering is the price of being alive," said folk singer Judy Collins.

What makes the Christian's lot better is the belief in a heaven to come. The apostle Paul wrote, "Though outwardly we are wasting away, yet inwardly we are being rewarded every day. For our light and momentary troubles are achieving for us an eternal glory that far outweighs them all" (2 Corinthians 4:17–18).

"If God disarmed every shooter and prevented every drunk driver from crashing, this would not be a real world in which people made consequential choices. It would not be a world of character development and faith development. It would not be a world where families put their arms around one another to face life's difficulties," wrote Christian author Randy Alcorn in *If God Is Good.*

Scholars believe the oldest book in the Bible is the book of Job. "This man was blameless and upright; he feared God and shunned evil" (Job 1:1). Job had seven sons and three daughters and owned more than one thousand livestock.

When Job praised the Lord, Satan was not impressed. Of course, Satan reasoned, Job prospered with everything a man of his time could want. The Lord then said to Satan, "Very well, then, everything he has is in your hands, but on the man himself do not lay a finger" (Job 1:12).

Calamity ensued. Enemies attacked and killed Job's oxen. Fire from the sky killed his sheep. An enemy stole his camels. Then a mighty wind struck the house where Job's ten children gathered, killing them all. Only several servants survived to tell Job the news.

Remarkably, Job did not blame God for any of this. Not yet. "The Lord gave and the Lord has taken away; may the name of the Lord be praised" (Job 1:21).

But Satan was not finished, and God permitted him to crank it up a notch. "[Job] is in your hands, but you must spare his life" (Job 2:6). Job's body was then covered from head to toe with painful sores. The pitiful Job made things worse by scraping the sores with pieces of broken pottery.

By then, Job had had it, cursing the day he was born. "Why did I not perish at birth, and die as I came from the womb?" (Job 3:11).

At a low point in his life, John Bunyan, author of *The Pilgrim's Progress*, wrote, "I was glad for the beasts, birds and fishes, for they did not have a sinful nature and were not subject to the wrath of God. They were not to go to hellfire after death, and I would have been glad if I were one of them."

The book of Job ends with Job acknowledging that the God who created the universe still rules the universe. "I know that you can do all things; no plan of yours can be thwarted" (Job 42:2).

Job's faithfulness was rewarded. He fathered seven more sons and three daughters. "Nowhere in all the land were there found women as beautiful as Job's daughters" (Job 42:15). His livestock was double what it had been before, and he gave us the book of Job.

"I used to think Satan *loved* suffering, that it was his weapon of choice against our faith," wrote Marshall Segal of DesiringGod.org. "But while he certainly (and viciously) tries to make the most of it, I now suspect Satan secretly hates suffering. He's simply seen it draw too many people closer to Christ."

At the age of thirty-two, I had delicate surgery to remove a tumor on my pituitary gland. The surgeon thought he had an accurate map of blood vessels in my skull, based on CT scans. He mistakenly severed a vessel, and removing the tumor had suddenly become job two. Job one was to stop the bleeding, which required an emergency transfusion of two units of blood. (Had I not survived the surgery, my parting words as I left this mortal coil would have been saying to the anesthesiologist, "Ninety-nine, ninety-eight.") When the surgery was complete, the doctor, who looked stunned after what had just happened, said to Donna, "Well, he's still alive."

I would spend one week recovering in the intensive care unit. One night around three in the morning, my roommate stopped breathing and died. That week, the words from Paul's New Testament letters took on fresh meaning. During those dark days, I read about suffering, about leaning on Jesus to provide strength. It all clicked.

Kayra Montanez, a member of the pastoral staff at Liquid

Church, left her career as an attorney in her native Puerto Rico to come with her husband, Jose, to New Jersey to obtain better services for their three-year-old son who was born with Down syndrome.

During the COVID-19 crisis, three Liquid Church pastors delivered online sermons in a series called "Dangerous Prayers." Montanez preached the third sermon, "Break My Heart!" based on the Old Testament story of Nehemiah.

Montanez declared, "What I'm talking about is the whole Gospel, which is a lot more than the idea that God exists to make your life better, to take away your pain, to fill you with blessings, to make you prosperous, and to make you comfortable. It is the opposite of 'If you can see it, you can be it, and if you can name it, you can claim it.' What I'm getting at here is that God's greatest blessings come from God's greatest breakings."

Montanez continued, "There are blessings on the other side of brokenness. So, ask Him, 'Break my heart.' And, church, never forget, when God breaks your heart, He promises to be close to you. Psalm 34:18, my favorite Bible verse. 'The Lord is close to'—let's say it together, church— 'the brokenhearted who are crushed in spirit."

In his book *If God Is Good,* Randy Alcorn wrote, "God might to say to us, 'I have intimate understanding of what it is to be in your place. You have no clue what it is to be in my place. If you'd experienced Gethsemane [where Jesus sweat drops of blood] and the march to Golgotha and the horrors of the Cross, you'd not question for a moment either my understanding or my love.'"

According to first-century historians, eleven of Jesus's twelve disciples died a martyr's death. The exception was John, who died in exile on an island, where he wrote the book of Revelation near the end of his life.

None of us wanted to be visiting our granddaughter in the hospital, but through all the suffering in her room and up and down the hallways in the PICU in Morristown and the children's hospital in New Brunswick, the presence of the Lord was there. Each day, Abby wrote an encouraging Bible verse on the whiteboard. "The steady calmness that Abby and Peter displayed day after day was amazing, while constantly encouraging Leah," said Peter's mother, Ann . "As so many people from the community came faithfully to encourage Leah and our family, Abby and Peter seemed to be a calm witness of God's loving control."

"Another blessing of this experience is how God has given a special gift of character to Leah, who has come through all the difficulties," said Peter's father, Art. "God has already used her for His purposes to glorify Him, encourage others in the power of prayer. Who knows what more He has in store for her, but we can be confident in His plans for Leah."

"God never promised that we wouldn't have troubles. He never promised that we wouldn't have sorrow and pain. He never promised that we would have a comfortable life. What He promised is that He would be with us no matter what," said Mark Kincade, pastor of Grace Alliance Church in Piscataway, the church Donna and I attend.

CHAPTER 6

The Capacity to Love

L eah Hansen may have won, as one doctor put it, the "bad lottery" when she suffered a rare spinal cord stroke. However—and clearly there is a conflict of interest here— she did win what C. S. Lewis might call the "heredity and environment" lottery. This includes her family, her church, and her community.

On July 1, 2006, at the historic Millington Baptist Church, our daughter Abigail Ann Malwitz married Peter Arthur Hansen, the son of Art and Ann Hansen. The two became one. Two families became more than one three years later, when Abby gave birth to Leah Rose Hansen. And then, over the next four years, the births of Timmy, Serena, and Joey.

In that image of the paralytic man being lowered to Jesus, where I imagine four guys holding four corners of an old sail— representing the family, the church, the community, and the medical community—it was the family that did the heavy lifting.

Abby and Peter met at Liquid Church in 2004, then a ministry designed for young people that met on Sunday evenings at the Millington church. They got to know each other on a church-sponsored ski trip to Upstate New York, after Peter had dropped plans to go skiing in British Columbia, Canada, to go with the church group. Abby was with a group of girlfriends when one of them, Jan Cerrigione, went up to Peter at a rest stop on the New York Thruway and told him, "You're going to be our friend."

After Peter graduated from Wheaton College in 2001, he returned to New Jersey and attended the church where he had been raised. He reasoned, "I've got to find a wife, and I'm not going to find one here." He then began attending Sunday evening services of Liquid Church, a congregation that had attracted scores of young adults. Abby learned about Liquid Church from her cousin Rachel Eck, and she also began attending.

A few months after the ski trip, following a church-sponsored whitewater rafting trip, Peter called his mother from the road, saying he would stop by the house in East Hanover, and there would be four girls with him. Ann suspected that Peter might have had a match in mind. When they left, Ann remembers saying to herself, "I think it's the tall one," referring to the five-foot-ten Abby Malwitz.

As soon as they started dating, Abby left the country. She had been accepted in a program for science teachers to study in Africa over the summer. She was excited to go, and unlike Peter, who called off a ski trip to British Columbia, she went to Kenya for three weeks. The relationship was resumed when she returned. "Then we started dating for real," said Peter. Following the wedding, they moved into a second-floor apartment in Madison, New Jersey.

In less than a year, they decided to plant roots, midway between their parents' homes and midway between their jobs. This venture was not for the financially squeamish. The search centered on Morris County, the twelfth wealthiest county in the nation, according to US News and World Report, and Somerset

County, the fifteenth wealthiest. They purchased a fixer-upper Cape Cod house in the Gillette section of Long Hill Township, in Morris County.

Peter's parents live about thirty minutes north, and Donna and I live about thirty minutes east. We have become close to Art and Ann, often sharing holiday meals with them. We traveled with them on church-sponsored trips to Israel in 2018, Egypt in 2020, and Greece and Italy in 2022. Before our flight to Egypt, the four of us had our picture taken at Dulles International Airport near Washington, DC. I told the kids there was a lot of inheritance about to lift off.

(We arrived home on March 3, 2020 in a filled-to-the-brim EgyptAir flight, not knowing the severity of COVID-19 that would soon put the country in lockdown in less than two weeks. We then understood why most Asian tourists wore masks on that flight from Cairo.)

The families' finest hour would be the first three months of Leah's illness, when twins Serena and Joey went to live at the Hansens' house, and Timmy to ours. "There was no plan. It just happened," said Art..

Peter recalled what he and Abby were thinking. "You guys are going to have to take the kids. We can't do it. You're going to have to figure it out. There was never a moment when we worried about the other three. We didn't have the capacity to miss them. We knew they missed us. It was nice to know we had people who had the capacity to love them."

The four grandparents were retired, in good health, and nearby. Peter also has two sisters, Elizabeth and Sarah, who were then living with Art and Ann. Abby's sister Carrie lived about three miles from Donna and me. The aunts would do anything for Leah and the other three kids.

Abby and Peter grew up in the church. Abby attended

Grace Alliance Church in Piscataway and the youth group at Evangelical Free Church of Montgomery. Peter grew up in the Calvary Evangelical Free Church in Essex Fells.

When Leah was in the fourth grade and studied the history of Ellis Island, it sparked our interest in helping her learn her families' origin stories. Leah's four grandparents—that would be my generation—were baby boomers. Her eight great-grandparents, the Greatest Generation, survived the Great Depression, experienced World War II, and grew baby boomer families in the New Jersey suburbs.

Two of Leah's great-grandfathers—Donna's father, Roger Johnson, and Art's father, Magne Hansen—saw combat in Europe, and both fought in the Battle of the Bulge. My father, Walter Malwitz, served in North Africa, Italy, France, and Germany, handling military mail. Ann's father, Kenneth Heisinger, suffered a severe leg injury as a twelve-year-old. Because of his injury, he did not serve in the military, though he did work as an electrician in the navy shipyards in New York Harbor, a role nearly as important as what the soldiers were doing in North Africa and Europe.

The Battle of the Bulge, in the winter of 1944–45, was a defining moment for the participants. Art said that his father made a pact with God during that bitter winter of war: If God spared him, he would never complain about anything for the rest of his life. "And," said Art, "he never complained about anything!"

Art grew up in the Calvary Evangelical Free Church in Orange, New Jersey, where a cluster of Norwegian immigrants settled, and Norwegian was spoken there. "Our church was the center of our family life," he said. Ann attended Brookdale Baptist Church in Bloomfield, which appealed to her parents because of its vibrant youth group.

Ann accepted Christ as her savior at an old-fashioned Methodist tent meeting in Caldwell. "I am so thankful for Christian parents and in-laws who prayed faithfully for us and our children. What a blessing. It's a privilege to now be able to pray for our children and grandchildren every day," she said.

Donna and her family attended Northfield Baptist Church in Livingston. I grew up at the Orchard Park Church of the Christian and Missionary Alliance (CMA) in Union. Art and Ann met at a church activity at Brookdale Baptist Church. Donna and I met at Long Hill Chapel, a CMA church in Chatham.

Art's parents and Ann's parents each had three children. My parents and Donna's parents each had five. Do the math. Sixteen baby boomers, raised in suburban New Jersey.

Art and Ann sent three children to Wheaton College, a Christian college near Chicago, and one to St. Elizabeth's College. Donna and I sent Abby and Carrie to Messiah College. The one kid among the two families to go to a secular university was our son, Andrew, who went to Massachusetts Institute of Technology, where his most important circle of friends were members of Campus Crusade for Christ. His wedding party included four alumni of MIT and Campus Crusade.

The Hansens have a second home adjacent to Camp of the Woods, a Christian camp in the Adirondack Mountains. We have a second home at the Jersey Shore, on property owned by the Ocean Grove Camp Meeting Association, the site of an historic Methodist campground.

All that to say the family holding one corner of that discarded old sail was robust and blessed, with deep roots in the church. As heartbroken as we were with an eight-year-old girl paralyzed and unable to breathe, we shared a common belief: we can do this because God can do this.

For three months, we roused Timmy in the morning for school and read to him at bedtime. I drove him to school, and we fought for access to my smartphone during the commute. He lobbied for video games. I struggled to get him to watch National Geographic specials about the Brazilian rain forest or whales in the South Pacific.

One day when Timmy was sick, the school nurse called Peter. I met Peter and Timmy at the pediatrician's office, where Timmy received a ten-day prescription for an antibiotic. He saw the medicine bottle, and he knew his numbers. "It says I have to stay out of school for ten days," he insisted. He missed only one day.

His aunt Carrie often arranged after-school playdates and transportation for Timmy. At the end of the three months, one of my favorite text messages was the one from Jacquie Petras, the mother of Jacob Petras, one of Timmy's after-school buddies. "I miss my Timmy," she wrote. Timmy often also went to Dylan Pudlak's house after school. "We loved having him. He had so much energy, and he was great for Dylan," said Kristin Pudlak, who made the two boys finish their homework before playtime.

Meanwhile, Art and Ann had twenty-four-hour days with preschoolers Serena and Joey. They took walks. The twins were enrolled in Imagine That, a creative indoor playground about two miles from the Hansen home. Ann brought the twins to meetings at church created for mommies and their preschoolers; Ann played the role of a young mommy again. Art brought Joey to church to participate in the men's group work projects. They arranged playdates with kids from church. "The busyness of taking care of the twins would take my mind off Leah. Otherwise, I would be worrying and thinking about her all the time," said Ann.

CHAPTER 7

Seats at the Table

In the spring of 2021, Donna and I binged our way through the Netflix series *Shtisel*. It told the story of several generations of Orthodox Jews living in modern Jerusalem and staying obedient to their Hebrew Bible, what Christians call the Old Testament.

In the final episode, Rabbi Shulem is sitting with his son and his brother, and he quotes philosopher Isaac Bashevis Singer: "The dead don't go anywhere. They're all here. Each man is a cemetery. An actual cemetery, in which lie all our grandmothers and grandfathers, the father and mother, the wife, the child. Everyone is here all the time."

Then, characters who died earlier in the series appeared, and the dining room banter continued as if the characters were all alive and well.

I do not think this is entirely fiction.

In Genesis 15:15, Abraham was told, "You, however, will go to your fathers in peace and be buried at a good old age." Genesis 49:33 tells the story of the death of Jacob: "He drew his feet up into bed, breathed his last and gathered to his people." When his infant son died, David said, "I will go to him, but he will not return to me" (2 Samuel 12:23).

There will be reunions in heaven. "Death breaks ties on earth but renews them in heaven," wrote Erwin W. Lutzer in *One Minute After You Die. A Preview of Your Final Destination*.

The Bible takes lineage seriously. The story is told how the descendants of Habaiah, Hakkoz, and Barzillai had the knowledge, the devotion, and the temperament to be priests, but they were barred. "These [three men] searched for their family records, but they could not find them and so were excluded from the priesthood as unclean" (Ezra 2:62). They could not prove they were in the line of priests descending from Aaron.

In the New Testament book of Matthew, the author records forty-two lines of descendants from Abraham to Joseph, the father of Mary. The author of Luke has seventy-seven lines of descent from Adam to another Joseph, the young man betrothed to Mary. Both genealogies converge with King David.

Before her death in 1983, my aunt Ruth Doerr was hospitalized in New York City and was attended to by a nurse with the last name Otis. When Aunt Rudie mentioned how her mother's maiden name was Alieta Otis, the nurse brought in his family tree that traced the Otis line in America to the 1620s. Aunt Rudie recognized some of the names and dates as her ancestors too.

My sister, Alieta Eck, later traced our Otis roots to Thomas Otis, who was born in Somersetshire, England, in 1530. The earliest record of an Otis in America was Stephen Otis, who was born in Somersetshire in 1578 and immigrated to America on a ship that would have taken three months to cross the Atlantic Ocean. He died in Scituate, Massachusetts, in 1635. (Let me pause to say your interest in my genealogy might be equal to my interest in your fantasy football team. This is for Leah and her siblings to understand where they came from.)

The Otis family would play a significant role in the

American Revolution. James Otis famously appeared before the Massachusetts Superior Court to argue against the British imposition of the Molasses Act, an onerous tax for the colonists. In the fourth hour of his argument, he declared, "Taxation without representation is tyranny." It was a rallying cry during the Revolutionary War. And it stuck. Today, an abbreviated version, "Taxation without Representation," adorns license plates of Washington, DC, residents, who have no voice in the United States Senate.

That day, Founding Father John Adams recalled, "[James] Otis was a flame of fire. American independence was then and there born."

His sister, Mercy Otis Warren, author of a three-volume history of the American Revolution, called her brother "the first champion of American freedom."

According to my sister Alieta, James and Mercy are Leah Hansen's second cousin, eight times removed. They would have seats at our *Shtisel* dining room table. Aviator Amelia Earhart's mother was an Otis, and she is on our family tree. (I hope to see her at the table and get the real story of her disappearance.)

Another James Otis was born in either 1704 or 1705 in West Barnstable, Massachusetts, and I mention him if only to cite the title of a book he authored: *The Rudiments of Latin Prosody with a Dissertation on Letters and the Principles of Harmony in Poetic and Prosaic Composition*. He died in 1783 when he was struck by lightning.

A name familiar to many is Elishu Otis, born in 1811. He was a craftsman who designed everything from industrial machines and sawmills to children's toys. He was working in Yonkers, New York, when he was commissioned to convert a sawmill into a bedstand factory. He thought there must be a better way to lower debris from higher floors and designed what he called a "safety hoist." Its new feature was a braking system. He began a company called Union Elevator Co., later Otis Brothers and Co. (The next time you walk in and out of an elevator, look for the Otis nameplate.)

Donna's side of the family, however, trumps mine. Putting dates and names into one of several commercial genealogy sites, I learned how my wife, born Donna Johnson, is in the same bloodline as George Washington.

George Washington and my wife, and Leah Hansen and her siblings, can trace their English roots to Ralph Neville, the first earl of Westmoreland, who was born in 1355 at Raby Castle in Dunham, England.

Loren Varga, a friend at church and the most serious genealogist I know, discovered how he and Donna are related through the Ralph Neville line. Loren traced that line back to Charlemagne; Sergius Paulus, who is mentioned in the Bible in Acts 13:7; the sister of King Nebuchadnezzar; Levi, a son of Jacob; and all the way back to Adam and Eve. That is where it ends.

These are stories of the bloodlines that formed Leah, with special emphasis to focus on Godly women.

CHAPTER 8

Godly Women

There will be two women in particular at that *Shtisel* table who had in common the penmanship of an extraordinary letter to one of their sons.

I already mentioned Mercy Otis Warren, called *The Muse of the Revolution,* the title of her biography by historian Nancy Rubin Stuart. She was a friend of John and Abigail Adams, Samuel Adams, and John Hancock. John Adams called her a "real genius," though her relationship with the third president soured when he did not think she gave him enough credit in her 1,200-page three-volume history of the American Revolution. She and her husband, James Warren, hosted numerous gatherings in her home with the bold-face names from the Revolutionary War era. She wrote, "By the Plymouth [Massachusetts] fireside were many political plans originated."

One night, George and Martha Washington were supposed to go to the Warrens' for dinner, but George was summoned to Rhode Island on military matters.

When Mercy completed her trilogy of the Revolutionary War in 1805, *History of the Rise of Progress and Termination of the American Revolution,* President Thomas Jefferson ordered copies for himself and members of his cabinet. The prickly John

Adams found his name on only four pages. He wrote ten letters to her, some twenty pages long. Adams huffed, "History is not the province of the ladies."

She was an early critic of the US Constitution because it did not grant Americans certain rights—no guarantees of a free press, freedom of conscience, or trial by jury. Warren complained that the Constitution didn't protect citizens from arbitrary warrants giving officials power to "enter our houses, search, insult, and seize at pleasure." Her public criticism contributed to the pressure that led Congress to pass the Bill of Rights in 1789.

In *The Women of the American Revolution*, published in 1848, author Elizabeth Ellet quoted a letter Mercy Otis Warren had written to one of her sons. Though she was self-educated, she spoke a formal king's English, and it requires careful reading:

> I am persuaded you will never counteract those native dictates that lead you to struggle for distinction by cherishing that ambition that dignifies the rational creature. May you extend your views beyond the narrow limits of time, that you may rank not only with those models of virtue and heroism that have been so much your admiration from your earliest youth, but may be able to stand with confidence before HIM who discriminates not according to the weak decisions of man, but by the unerring scale of eternal truth.

From across the Atlantic Ocean came another godly woman. Olga Sturm, my paternal grandmother, arrived at Ellis Island in 1900 at the age of eighteen. Ferdinand Malwitz had come through Ellis Island in 1892, and he was told to look after Olga, who was twelve years younger than he. She settled in Brooklyn, and he was living in Union, New Jersey. According to the story I was told, she felt bad about how long it took him to get back and forth to Brooklyn. So she proposed, "Let's get married."

English was her second language, so that a letter she wrote to my father, Walter Malwitz, in 1934, the year he graduated from Union High School, does not have the poetic cadence of the King's English.

> To Walter, "Blessed are the pure in heart for they shall see God. Matthew 5:8. All you are has long been placed upon the altar, for God would not be satisfied with less. He'll give you purity of heart and satisfy you with living water. Because His love for you is great and you he wants to bless, be true and faithful to the call of God within your heart. Like Abraham of old, like David at the fold, today Jesus is speaking: Come unto me and rest. He always only speaks to faithfulness, the called out few. His blood which He applied upon your heart, a sign you've been chosen, too! Be not afraid, when others mock and dark and stormy clouds appear for you, sufficient is his grace. May Jesus, the Son of God, your friend and Savior dear enfold and shelter you till soon you'll meet him face to face. In love, your mother.

Olga Sturm Malwitz was a woman of strong faith. My aunt Helen Malwitz lived briefly with my grandparents at their home on Vauxhall Road in Union. She told the story of how she heard Grandma Malwitz praying in the next room, in her native German. Aunt Helen remembered her praying for her children, her children's children, her children's children's children, and their best friends. That would be prayers for my father's generation, my generation, and Abby's.

This prayer has been answered many times over, with scores of her progeny serving the Lord today. As for her children's children's best friends, I suggest she was praying for Eric Vieth, a close friend from high school who joined me on road trips to Florida, Crosley Field in Cincinnati, and Dyess Air Force Base in Abilene, Texas, where I dropped him off on Labor Day weekend in 1971. He would settle in the Abilene area after serving in Vietnam. As an adult, he became a born-again Christian, and today, he is an active member in his congregation.

Both Mercy Otis Warren and Olga Sturm Malwitz knew suffering. Warren had five children. Three preceded her in death, and a fourth had his leg amputated after being wounded in a Revolutionary War naval battle. She wrote, "The waves have rolled over me, the billows repeatedly broken over me, yet I am not sunk down. Shall I complain that I have never been suffered to catch the last accents of my dying friends and children? No. *He who knoweth my frame, knoweth what is fittest for me.*" (emphasis mine).

My grandmother Olga Sturm Malwitz also knew suffering. Two of her daughters died seven days apart from diphtheria in 1915. Anna Malwitz was twelve. Elisia Malwitz was eleven. (Diphtheria also caused the death of Elishu Otis, the inventor of the elevator. He was forty-nine.)

My cousin Elaine Malwitz Thomas remembers how her mother, my aunt Helen, got into vigorous arguments with our grandmother. Who knows what divided them? Aunt Helen was a formidable student of the Bible and everybody's favorite Sunday school teacher. Elaine remembers how occasionally the going got tough when the two argued. "I remember poor Grandpa asking my mother to be gentle. 'Don't forget she lost two children.'"

Grandma Olga was a devout Pentecostal. "I can recall her trying desperately to get me to speak in tongues, which I found rather frightening and strange," said Elaine. "I loved Grandpa. I was rather fearful of Grandma."

Who knows how much my grandmother may have blamed herself for the deaths of her two daughters?

When Elaine was in the second grade, she fell on her way to school, suffered severe internal injuries, and missed three months of class. "Grandma would come into my bedroom and ask what sin I was not confessing since God was not healing me. I was eight years old," said Elaine. Leah was in third grade when she suffered a spinal cord stroke, and she also missed three months of school. Believe me, if anyone had gone into Leah's hospital room and asked her what sins she was not confessing, there would have been punches thrown. (Looking at you, Peter.)

Following the deaths of Anna and Elisia, my grandmother gave birth to my father, Walter, and my uncle Eddie. The two of them were close, strong believers, pillars in their church, and in every sense of the word, gentlemen.

My cousin Elise Malwitz Henrichs recalled, "More than once, I heard the story of Ed choking on hard candy and his mother declaring, 'Well, he's gone.' Walter, however, turned his brother upside down, shaking him until he expelled the candy. My dad always felt he owed his life to his brother and remembered that Walter continually watched out for him. Perhaps your dad's vibrant faith was the model our dad followed. I know my dad loved God first, then my mother, then his three girls. How blessed we all are to have had such fathers."

Elaine recalled, "I remember Grandpa as a gentle,

hardworking farmer, getting up at four in the morning to milk the cows, taking long naps in the afternoon, and finishing the day milking the cows and cleaning barns. He would never drive anything with a motor. Though your dad and my dad bought him a tractor, he would never use it. I recall riding next to Grandpa on a horse-drawn carriage hauling grain for the cows on Route 22, with lines of cars behind us, which Grandpa declared were in too much of a hurry."

Mercy Otis Warren is in the history books. "A fascinating reminder," wrote Christine Kreiser of *American History* magazine, "that the ideals of independence resonated as strongly with American women as with American men."

The only known written history of Olga Sturm Malwitz is right here. Abby was also blessed with two grandmothers who lived long enough to see her go away to college. They, too, were familiar with grief.

Donna's mother, Agnes Robertson Johnson, traced her roots to Renfrewshire, a fishing village in Scotland. When Agnes was nine years old, her mother died, and she would be raised by an aunt. Her faith journey began at the Methodist Church in Roseland, New Jersey, where she met Roger Johnson of Livingston. They were married in 1941. One year later, they were separated when Roger joined the military, serving in combat in World War II, where he was awarded two Purple Hearts.

In 1968, their second-oldest child, Joyce Johnson, was killed by a drunk driver. "They leaned heavily on their faith in a loving God and a future eternity with her," said Donna.

Tragedy struck Agnes again in 1989 when she suffered a crippling stroke; that was one reason the diagnosis of Leah having a stroke was so alarming. Roger Johnson's finest hour was the way he cared for his wife the final six years of her life, until her death in an automobile accident.

The line of godly women would include my mother, Virginia Doerr Malwitz. She was born in Chicago, the fifth child of George and Alieta Doerr. George was a successful businessman with a home in the tony Chicago suburb of Wilmette. (The handsome six-bedroom house where she grew up was valued by Zillow at $1.47 million in 2021.)

When my mother was nine, her father died on Christmas Eve in 1926. Three years later, the stock market crashed, and the country fell into the Great Depression. Alieta Otis Doerr, now a single mother, moved to New Jersey. Virginia graduated fifth in her class at Battin High School, then the all-girls public high school in Elizabeth, at a time when the best and brightest girls had three career options: secretary, nurse, or teacher. She became a secretary.

She met Walter Malwitz at a Pentecostal church in Elizabeth, but plans for marriage were stalled by World War II. He was stationed at Fort Sam Houston in San Antonio, Texas, when he proposed long-distance. She took the train from Elizabeth, and after the train picked up passengers in St. Louis, she struck up a conversation with an oil executive from Texas who had gone to St. Louis for the 1942 World Series. He heard her story—how she was going to San Antonio to marry a soldier—and treated her to dinner in the dining car. She later realized she could have ordered anything from the menu, and the oilman would have gladly paid. Instead, she ordered something modest and regretted it the rest of her life. "I should have ordered the Porterhouse."

Walter and Virginia were married at the chapel at Fort Sam Houston by a chaplain whom my father had befriended. The wedding needed one witness, so the chaplain summoned the pianist who was practicing for the next day's Sunday service. What my mother remembers is that the pianist was wearing pin curlers in her hair.

She remained for several weeks in Texas before heading home, and one of my biggest regrets is not knowing the rest of the story. My father had a car while in Texas; when and where and how he got a car as a soldier is not the biggest mystery. The greater mystery is how my mother drove that car from San Antonio to Elizabeth in 1942.

The car did not have a spare tire, and the top halves of the headlights were not blackened, a requirement during the war as part of blackout restrictions. There were no interstate highways. There were no chain hotels or motels, no cell phones, no GPS, and no credit cards. What route did she take? Where did she stay? *When we meet at that table, your Ricky has questions.*

After the war, they settled down in Union and began having their Baby Boomer children, in 1946, 1948, 1951, 1955, and 1958. Our father worked at the post office in Union, and my mother was a full-time mom.

Sometime in the early 1950s, she started feeling everyday pain. She was diagnosed with rheumatoid arthritis. She would have numerous operations, with artificial joints eventually placed in her ankles, knees, and hands. Her shoes had to be specially crafted. Getting up in the morning was difficult. Making lunch for school was our job. I never knew her to not be in pain.

In the early years of their marriage my parents attended a Pentecostal church in Elizabeth, but when she began suffering from arthritis, members of the church suggested the reason my mother was in so much pain was because she was not praying hard enough. It was time to find another church. A man who worked with my father at the post office invited him to visit the Christian and Missionary Alliance Church in Cranford. They went, and for the rest of their lives, they attended CMA churches in Cranford, Union, and Chatham. I met Donna at the CMA church in Chatham, and we were founding members in the mid-1980s of the CMA church in Piscataway, where we worship today.

Mercy Otis Warren, Olga Sturm Malwitz and Virginia Doerr were godly women who wrestled with suffering, trusted the Lord and passed their DNA onto Leah. So was also blessed with the DNA from her maternal grandmother Donna and paternal grandmother Ann, who Leah christened Nana and Mama respectively.

CHAPTER 9

Bright Hope for Tomorrow

Some readers own this part of the story. They may have known Leah Hansen personally, may have heard her story from others or seen it on a prayer chain and then prayed for the eight-year-old girl who was lying paralyzed in a hospital bed with a mysterious illness.

Writing in a different context, the Old Testament prophet Malachi said of God: "See if I will not throw open the floodgates of heaven and pour out so much blessing that you will not have enough room for it" (Malachi 3:10). Malachi was writing about tithing and storehouses.

This is about Leah and the floodgates of healing, and in God's economy, floodgates of prayer matter. "The design of God in thus uniting people in praying for each other when in affliction or danger, is that deliverance may be matter of common gratulations and praise," wrote Princeton Seminary theologian Charles Hodge (1797–1878). "Thus, all hearts are drawn out to God and Christian fellowship is promoted."

Praying for Leah was an act of fellowship. Answered prayer was shared joy. I recall being at a Liquid Church service when a woman visiting from Canada was introduced to Leah and was excited to see answered prayer standing in front of her. "Oh, you're the girl I've been praying for."

As people learned about the little girl hospitalized with serious symptoms, a common reaction in phone calls, emails, and social media was the promise of prayer. On social media, it was often followed with an emoji of clasped hands. What else could you do? Abby and Peter did not need childcare for Leah's siblings. They did not need casseroles. But who could not pray?

Prayer requests circled the globe. My brother Nelson founded The Finishers Project, now known as Mission Next, an organization that helps people from my generation find opportunities to serve in foreign missions. He spread the prayer request to people from the Middle East to the South Pacific. People in China were praying. A former newspaper colleague said she would be praying north of the Arctic Circle.

My favorite prayer story involved a Marriott Hotel reservations clerk; God knows her name. That first week in March 2018, Donna and I and my brother Nelson and his wife, Marge, were planning to stay at a Marriott in the Orlando area for three nights, while attending the Ligonier National Conference in Orlando. Then Leah had her spinal cord stroke.

Donna called Marriott to cancel our reservations and told the clerk why. The clerk said, "I believe in a God who is in the healing business. What's the name of your granddaughter?"

"Leah," said Donna.

The 1-800 Marriott woman abruptly said, "I'm going to pray for her right now." Before getting down to business, she prayed for Leah by name, over the phone.

Prayer seems quite easy. You clear your mind as best you can and then either silently or verbally tell God you adore Him, thank Him for your daily bread, and make your requests known, as if the Creator of the universe is interested in *you*. If

His eye is on that sparrow, He can still hear your prayer. If it is so simple, how then do I explain the collection of books in my library? *Prayer. Does It Make a Difference?* by Philip Yancey. *Prayer. Experiencing Awe and Intimacy with God* by Timothy Keller. *Handle with Prayer* by Charles Stanley. *The Weapon of Prayer* by David D. Ireland. Among others.

If I peek into your library and find a half dozen books on dieting or golf, I figure I know what your challenges are. You want to slim down or improve your iron game, or both. That might explain why there are books by Yancey et al. on my shelves. They are all helpful. Like the weekend golfer who hopes just one more book will help, these authors are helpful guides for Christians who consider their prayer life weaker than it should be.

"If our prayer is meager, it is because we believe it to be supplemental, and not fundamental," Alistair Begg said on a Truth for Life podcast that aired August 4, 2020. "If you're like me, of all the things that we don't want anyone else to find out about, in relationship to our spiritual pilgrimage, it is how little we pray."

A speaker in Ocean Grove in the summer of 2022, Vito Aiuto, pastor of the Renaissance Church in Springfield, New Jersey, said "Nobody says their prayer life is where it should be." (I surveyed the room and we all seemed to be nodding in agreement.).

In his book, Keller writes, "Prayer is the way to experience a powerful confidence that God is handling our lives well, that our bad things will turn out for good, our good things cannot be taken from us, and the best things are yet to come."

Yancey tells the story of a "grief pastor" at a large church in Colorado. "Evangelicals tend to want to get to the happy ending," the grief pastor said. "Sometimes there is no happy ending, and we're simply suspended in grief. When I'm with suffering people, I feel like a deep-sea diver accompanying them to the depths. Come up too fast, and you'll decompress. We need to stay with the grief for a while, feel it, let it out. Maybe we can see things through tears we can't see dry-eyed."

This must have rung true to visitors who came to Leah's room in the first few days and weeks. Grief. Suffering. Tears. "The Bible does not rush to a happy ending," Yancey writes. "We need feel no guilt over such prayers of frustration, for God welcomes them."

King David wrote, "My life is consumed by anguish and my years by groaning; my strength fails because of my affliction, and my bones grow weak" (Psalm 31:10). Understand now, this is from the pen of Lord-is-my-shepherd David. His life ranges from "bones grow weak" to "lie down in green pastures," from "affliction" to "still waters."

The Bible devotes one of its sixty-six books to a book with the title Lamentations. It lives up to its billing, though the most well-known verses in the book are Lamentations 3:23–24, "Because of the Lord's great love, we are not consumed, for his compassions never fail. They are new every morning, great is your faithfulness."

Thomas Obediah Chisholm was a hymn writer who died in Ocean Grove in 1960. (I like to imagine he was at that service in the Great Auditorium in 1956 when Billy Graham spoke and I made a public profession of faith.) Chisholm wrote one of the most powerful hymns: "Great Is Thy Faithfulness." In the third verse, he wrote, "Strength for today and bright hope for tomorrow." This line rallied many of us during Leah's hospitalization and gave our prayers a focus: Strength for today. Bright hope for tomorrow.

The preceding verses in Lamentations give that hymn

context and serve as reminders of how God got us through. "I remember my affliction and my wandering, the bitterness and the gall. I will remember them, and my soul is downcast within me. Yet this I call to mind, and therefore I have hope" (Lamentations 3:19–23). The author then writes, "Because of the Lord's great love we are not consumed."

Dr. David Martyn Lloyd-Jones (1899-1981), author of *Studies in the Sermon on the Mount*, wrote of prayer: "It is the highest activity of the human soul, and therefore it is at the same time the ultimate test of a man's spiritual condition. There is nothing that tells the truth about us as Christian people so much as our prayer life."

The concept of talking to the God who created the universe and turning into a pray-without-ceasing lifestyle comes easier for some, including friends who told me three years later they were still praying for Leah. We are compelled to pursue God. He wants us to approach Him in prayer. He wants to hear from us every day.

When my father served in World War II in North Africa and Europe, he headed up a team of military postal workers, handling mail to and from soldiers. He took advantage of his access to the postal system to write often to my mother, then living in Elizabeth. They numbered their back-and-forth letters, from about the time he enlisted to when he returned, and the numbers were around one thousand. And do you suppose a letter was the highlight of the day? Even when they had next to nothing to say, it was a highlight. (I read some of the letters my father sent; sometimes he had nothing to say.)

God wants to hear from us and covets our prayers as much as my parents coveted those letters.

When I was working at the newspaper, we had a room in the office that was typically empty when not used to conduct private interviews. One time, I knocked, did not hear an answer, opened the door, and there was a new member of the staff, a woman, kneeling in prayer. *Oops, sorry.* My editor explained that when the woman, a Muslim, joined the staff, she asked if she could have access to a private space to pray at noon, and he offered her the room. (I never asked my editor if I could have private space to pray during work hours.)

If there is one thing to admire about the Islamic religion, it is the habit of scheduled prayer among devoted believers. Five times a day, Muslims are to bow in the direction of Mecca and pray. In our travels to the Middle East, we sometimes heard loudspeakers in major cities with the singsong call to prayer. While many Muslims will pray simply out of a sense of obligation, the fact is they are praying!

Has the volume of prayers that circled the globe made a difference in the recovery of Leah, especially the intense prayers by those closest to her? Her recovery from a spinal cord stroke has been on the high end of the recovery spectrum. Yes, I believe the persistence of prayer was a major factor.

Jesus tells the story of a woman who has been labeled "the persistent widow," who kept asking a judge to give her justice against her adversary. She was pestering. "This widow keeps bothering," said the judge. "I will see that she gets justice, so that she won't eventually come out and attack me! And the Lord said, 'Listen to what the unjust judge says. And will not God bring about justice for his chosen ones, who cry out to him day and night? Will he keep putting them off?'" (Luke 18:5–6).

Our cry day and night was not for justice but for healing. We persisted like a band of persistent widows.

A friend of mine told me he was raised with the belief that feeding-the-five-thousand-type miracles ceased after the New Testament age. Now he was praying daily for Leah, asking for a "big thing," a miracle. It was OK to pray for small things, he told me, like a parking space at the mall, but something as big as the *Talitha Koum* miracle in Mark 5:41? Perhaps, that was for Jesus and the first-century apostles.

Then came Leah. She wiggled her right toes. Then she kicked a softball ball with her right leg. Then she could breathe on her own. Then walk. Then play softball, ski, and join the cross-country team. My friend said he now prays for big things.

About a week after I spoke to that friend, I went to Newark Liberty International Airport to pick up my son Andrew, his wife, Elizabeth, and their son, Walter. It was a few days before Christmas, and the airport parking lot was overflowing. I had never before asked God to help me find a parking spot, not a big thing but a little thing – a parking space.

Bingo! I didn't even have time to say amen, when about fifty feet in front of me, I saw a welcoming set of white backup lights brighten near the terminal entrance. It was as if God, in the busyness of the holiday season, was finding a coveted parking spot at the airport for a grandfather who prayed a little prayer. Another Christmas miracle!

In the summer of 2022 Leah's brother Joey, then nine, was to play in the championship game in local baseball league. He asked Abby, "Is it OK to pray before a game, like ask God that I win?"

I loved it. His ask suggested that he believes in a God who is there and that God takes requests from a little left-hander. Joey pitched the final inning in a 14–10 victory.

CHAPTER 10

Miracles

W hen Abby graduated from Messiah College, she, like many fresh college graduates, decided to spend some time saving the world. She was accepted into the AmeriCorps program, which I describe to people of my generation as the domestic Peace Corps. She was given her first choice of an assignment, in Nashville, Tennessee, where she would counsel teenage girls in the public school system. Because the pay was so low that she qualified for food stamps, she took a part-time job with a company that assigned ushers to work at concerts and sporting events.

On January 8, 2000, she was at field level, ushering Tennessee Titans fans out of the stadium soon after the Buffalo Bills took a 16–15 lead with sixteen seconds remaining in the National Football League playoff game. The Bills would kick off to the Titans, and the game would soon be over. Discouraged fans were leaving the stadium in droves, to beat the traffic.

The Bills' kickoff went to the Titans' Lorenzo Neal, who lateraled the ball to Frank Wycheck, who then threw a backward pass across the field to Kevin Dyson, who was on the field only because two regulars were sidelined with injuries. Dyson ran seventy-five yards for a score, and the Titans went ahead, 21–16, and won the game.

Now, ushers had to obey orders and tell fans they could not return to the stadium they had recently abandoned. "Tough luck, pal. You gave up on the Titans." The play is known as the Music City Miracle.

Was it really a miracle?

An assistant coach for the Titans had seen the play work in a 1982 college football game. The Titans planned the play, practiced it, and the play worked. Was it luck? Yes. But as has been said, luck is the residue of design.

Prominent atheist Richard Dawkins, author of *The Blind Watchmaker. Why the Evidence of Evolution Reveals a Universe without Design*, wrote, "Events that we commonly call miracles are not supernatural but are part of a spectrum of more-or-less improbable natural events. A miracle, in other words, if it occurs at all, is a tremendous stroke of luck."

To be a true Christian, I assert, you must accept the miracles recorded in the Bible: that God created the universe by His Word, that Jesus of Nazareth was born to a virgin, that the sacrifice of sinless Jesus on the cross provided for the salvation of believers, and that Jesus conquered death in the resurrection. These are known as fundamentals of the faith.

There is division among evangelical Christians as to whether miracles like ones performed by Jesus and the apostles take place today, such as Jesus raising from the dead the daughter of the synagogue ruler. People on both sides of the debate agree that miracles described in the Bible are true—Jesus turning water into wine, healing ten lepers on the spot, feeding five thousand with a little boy's bag lunch.

Many believe that miracles ceased when the age of the first-century apostles ended and the Bible was complete, leaving no need for fresh revelation. Others believe miracles continue today.

In his book The Case for Miracles, author Lee Strobel wrote, I did agree with pastor and author Timmothy Keller, who said, 'There is nothing about miracles if a Creator God exists. If a God exists who is big enough to create the universe in all its complexity and vastness why should a mere miracle be such a mental stretch.'"

Strobel stated that miracles are more commonplace outside the Western world, spurring church growth recently in places like Brazil, China and the continent of Africa. Christian philosopher J.P. Moreland, reported Strobel, "Explained that out-breakings of the supernatural tend to occur in areas where there's leading-edge evangelism into cultures. A major factor in the current revival in the Third World is intimately connected to signs and wonders.'"

"If we could collect all the authentic stories all over the world—from all the missionaries and all the saints in all the countries of the world—if we collect the millions of encounters between Christians and demons and Christians and sickness and all the so-called coincidences of the world, we would be stunned. We would think we were living in a world of miracles, which we are," wrote John Piper.

When I was about ten years old, Edith Hansen, then a bookkeeper at the Christian and Missionary Alliance (CMA) national headquarters on 44th Street in Manhattan, came to our church in Union to work with young people. After serving fifty years in missions in Indonesia, she told me, "Yes, I agree with the occurrence of miracles happening when God is moving by His spirit in new places, new ways and to new people. Do we limit the Spirit's activity? Are we skeptical and not open to whatever God wants to do? I'm not sure. But I do know that new believers had more of the Spirit's moving in their lives."

Albert S. Simpson (1843–1919), founder of the CMA,

believed miracles never ceased, that they continued after the first century and the completion of the Bible. "If there is an essential difference between the apostolic and a later age, then the church is not one body but two. If we are the same body, we have the same life and power," he wrote in *The Gospel of Healing*.

In his twenties, Simpson suffered what today might be labeled a nervous breakdown. His congregation thought him to be "delicate." One day, he hiked up a mountain in New Hampshire, which required him to conquer his fear of heights. There, he had what he considered a mountaintop experience.

"The wolf and the Shepherd walked on either side, but the blessed Shepherd did not let me turn away. I pressed closer, closer, closer to His bosom and every step seemed stronger. When I reached that mountaintop, I seemed to be at the gate of heaven, and the world of weakness and fear was lying at my feet." His ministry flourished. The global impact of his life is being felt today. I began attending CMA churches nine months before I was born and help fund its global mission. However, this miracle took place in the heart of Simpson. It certainly did not have the visuals of ten lepers being healed by Jesus.

The experiences many of us had during Leah's illness and recovery took us from the mountain to the valley and back up to a mountaintop. God listened to our prayers. God healed. He empowered doctors, nurses, and therapists. *Soli Deo gloria*. To God be the glory.

We prayed from the start that Leah would be healed, and we clearly understood that first week that it was going to take the hand of God—working through the hands of medical professionals—to make her better. *Talitha Koum*. "Little girl, I say to you, 'Get up.'" We coveted supernatural help.

There were, as Richard Dawkins might put it, tremendous

strokes of luck along the way. Leah suffered her spinal cord stroke in the twenty-first century and would rely on medical equipment and expertise that did not exist when her mother was Leah's age. Abby took her to the ER that Monday night, instead of putting Leah to bed at home, where she would not have survived the night.

"In America, we have a lot of sophisticated medical technology, which is God's gift to us, and we should use it. That's the way He typically brings healing," Craig Keener told Strobel. Keener is the author of the book *Miracles* that tips the scale at 1,200 pages.

No natural laws were suspended one Saturday afternoon when Donna and I were traveling to Connecticut. We were at the peak of the Tappan Zee Bridge over the Hudson River when a hose burst on my car. I coasted to a convenience store with gas pumps up front, near the base of the bridge. They did not do repairs, but a clerk gave me several gallons of water to refill my radiator and directed me to a tire store a few blocks away where someone might be able to help.

A man who worked at the tire store explained the repair business was shut for the weekend and offered to let me park my car there until Monday morning. At a car wash across the street, a man who worked at the tire store saw steam coming from my engine and came to see what he could do to help. He volunteered to go to an auto parts store he thought might have a replacement hose. It did. He replaced the hose and filled the radiator with coolant. He charged me $119 and said I should go to my mechanic Monday morning to check out his work. On Monday, my mechanic called it a job well done and apologized for having recently replaced one hose but not the hose that failed and offered to write me a check for $119.

I called the tire store on Monday and asked to speak to the

boss, to thank him. We got to talking, and because he had an accent, I asked where he was from. The Dominican Republic, he said. Where in the DR? "La Vega."

La Vega! I had been with a group called Meeting God in Missions on six mission trips to La Vega, a city far from the DR beaches and not known for tourism. The tire store boss from La Vega was now active at a Baptist church in the Bronx. He loves Jesus just like we do. Do the math. The hose burst at the crest of the Tappan Zee Bridge, allowing me to coast forward. The tire store was closed for the weekend, but the man at the car wash saw our need. The nearby auto parts store had the hose in stock. The boss was from La Vega. My mechanic offered to cover the cost.

Nothing supernatural happened here. But how could I not see God's providence in the "improbable natural events" that Saturday-afternoon episode? The Tappan Zee miracle.

One of my favorite movies is O, Brother Where Art Thou, a whimsical story, accompanied by wonderful music, about three escapees from a Mississippi chain gang. Their aim is to uncover a treasure buried near the childhood home of one of the escapees, Ulysses Everett McGill, before the land it sits on is to be flooded as part of a project to build a hydroelectric dam.

When escapees Everett, Delmar, and Pete arrived at Everett's home, the sheriff was there waiting to capture them, hang them, and bury them in freshly dug graves. As the nooses were being put in place, Everett, played by George Clooney, got religion. He prayed the sinner's prayer. "I'm sorry that I turned my back on You, Lord. Please forgive me, and help us, Lord, and I swear I'll mend my ways."

Suddenly, a wave appeared, the hollow was flooded, and in the next scene the escaped prisoners bobbed up to the surface of the water. They were saved.

"A miracle! It was a miracle!" said a grateful Delmar.

"We prayed to God, and He pitied us," said Pete.

"Nothing doing," said Everett. "It just never fails. Once again, you two hayseeds are showin' how much you want for intellect. There's a perfectly scientific explanation for what just happened," said Everett.

Everett prayed for a miracle. Then circumstances worked in his favor, and Everett could explain the circumstances. Turns out there was no need for God after all, he figured. Sorry to have bothered You, Man Upstairs.

Several years ago, I attended a baseball game in Pittsburgh where between innings they used the jumbo screen to entertain the fans, with such staples as blooper plays and the awkward kiss cam. In the middle of one inning, they posted a video where four members of the Pirates were asked, "If you could go back in history and witness one event, what would it be?" One knucklehead chose a WrestleMania event. Another chose Game Seven of the 1960 World Series played a few miles away at Forbes Field. Then one player chose Jesus's resurrection, and the fourth player would have loved to see Jesus heal a blind man. (I would have loved to be there when Jesus fed the five thousand.)

There are three accounts of Jesus healing a blind man, in the books of Matthew, Mark, and John. In the story that takes up the entire ninth chapter of John, opponents of Jesus thought Him a sinner for healing on the Sabbath and then mocked the man who was healed: "You were steeped in sin at birth, how dare you lecture us?" (John 9:34).

"One thing I do know," the man told them, "I was blind but now I see!" (John 9:25).

This one thing we know. Leah entered the emergency room a quadriplegic and soon could not breathe. Now she skis, rides a bike, and runs track.

Leah's first day back at Liquid Church after her stroke, June 2018

Leah's baptism in Ocean Grove, June 2019

CHAPTER 11

Church Being the Church

A bout three o'clock in the morning on March 6, 2018, Peter sent an email to Josh and Sara Gill at their home in Bridgewater. He would have sent a text message but did not want to wake them in the middle of the night with an annoying ding. "Something happened," Peter wrote. "We're not sure what's going on with Leah. She can't move her limbs."

Several hours later, Abby sent Sara a text. "Leah wasn't able to breathe. I thought my daughter was going to die right in front of me."

"We prayed for Leah. We prayed for Abby and Peter. We prayed for the doctors," said Sara.

That afternoon, Sara would become part of the Liquid Church family that would help the Hansens. Abby's sister Carrie brought seven-year-old Timmy to the Gills' home, where he would play with eight-year-old Luke and seven-year-old Matthew. Sara remembers, "Leah was in the hospital, and Timmy, in a childish way, said to the boys, 'Let's go play Nerf guns.' He was aware Leah wasn't feeling well and was in the hospital. He was worried about his sister but didn't know how to process it."

About ten o'clock that morning, Peter called Jon Coords,

the pastor of the Somerville campus of Liquid Church. Coords remembered Peter telling him, "'Something happened last night.' Pete's an engineer. He wants to fix it, get the facts. He was really a rock. He gave me his data points."

But Peter was not without emotion. "He had his moments," said Jon, who went to the hospital later in the day. "That day was gut-wrenching. I don't know if I have ever been in a situation like that. And I wasn't the father.

"As a minister, I fight the urge to give an answer, try to solve the problem. My role at that time is to be present, encouraging. But not giving any false hope, telling him, 'This is going to get better.' You can't make those promises."

Coords said there were promises that Peter and Abby could lean on: "God is real. God loves us all more than we can possibly imagine. God is going to use this for His glory, in His timing. We weep with those who weep, mourn with those who mourn. There were many tears shed, lots of prayers."

In that room in the pediatric intensive care unit at Morristown Medical Center, Coords laid hands on Leah, "asking for supernatural intervention, right there at that moment, praying, 'Not my will but Thy will be done,' yielding to God that He has a plan. He sees the full tapestry of what is happening. You always have to have this kingdom mindset, this eternal mindset.

"We want it fixed now for her to be OK. If she was walking out of the hospital on Wednesday like nothing had ever been wrong, we wouldn't have known what happened. But because of the timing, God has been glorified. People that don't know Jesus know that something has happened, that this is a family of faith, that this family has a church that was praying on a massive scale," said Coords, now the lead pastor of One Church in Somerville.

"Leah's a walking testimony, a literal testimony to God's goodness. I don't know how many people visited her. They got to see Peter and Abby specifically. They saw the brokenness and pain. They also saw God move all the same. This is a beautiful faith story."

"When we heard about Leah, there was a footrace to get to Peter and Abby. Not with solutions but prayer and the gift of presence," said Tim Lucas, the lead pastor of Liquid Church. Tim has known Abby and Peter since 2004 when Liquid Church was in its infancy and Peter was one of the first keyboard players for the worship team. This was before the congregation grew from a single Sunday-evening service to a multisite church with eight campuses in New Jersey.

"Peter's a man's man—you know that. When I saw his face [in the hospital], I will never forget it. The word is *stricken*, the look of grief, heartsickness. I just started crying. I thought of my own kids. We just hugged, and he wept, and I wept, and we hugged."

Tim remembered having sat in his car outside the hospital, praying and wondering what he was about to see. "As a pastor, I don't know what I'm walking into. I had heard the bare bones. People didn't know exactly what had happened. 'What do you mean Leah's paralyzed?'

"For whatever reason, I remembered that Aramaic phrase. *Talitha Koum.* 'Little girl, arise.' I remembered hearing a message on that when I was little. I preached on that. Sometimes Jesus just healed with a word. 'Get up.' Sometimes he spat on some mud and healed a blind man. There never was a formula. 'Lord, I'm going to pray just what You prayed.' That little girl [whom Jesus healed] just got up. I remember praying that with Peter. I just prayed God's Word back to Him."

This was just the start. Liquid Church, as a body of believers, became part of the story. Remember that image of four guys holding four corners of an old sail, lowering the paralytic to Jesus through a hole in the roof? The family held one corner. Liquid Church held another.

"People in the church caught the feeling. There was a visceral compassion for Leah because she is such a ray of sunshine. And they love Peter and Abby. The church is at its best when we are caring for people. What people want to know: 'Does this place have legs outside of Sunday morning?'" said Pastor Tim.

"I like to say, 'We go to chapel on Sunday. We go to church the rest of the week,'" said Linda Hagg, whose husband, Dr. Gregg Hagg, was pastor of Mountainside Gospel Chapel when it donated its church property to Liquid Church in 2014.

Liquid Church had previously planned a praise and prayer meeting at their broadcast center in Parsippany for that Wednesday night, forty-eight hours after Leah became sick. Peter came forward, and the staff laid their hands on him. "Peter's bawling. I'm draped over him, bawling," Jon Coords remembered. "Even though He did not heal her in those moments, He did heal her."

The next Sunday, Donna and I brought our Timmy to the Somerville campus so he could be at church in a familiar environment. We had been to enough Liquid Church gatherings that many members recognized us and assured us they felt our pain. Inside the door of the Somerville Middle School, where the congregation was then meeting, Dawn Awan, one of the greeters, said encouraging words. I do not remember what they were, but they were the right words. Coords would lead the congregation in prayer at the end of the service, inviting Donna and me to the front of the auditorium. We knew we were with family.

A few weeks later, the Liquid Church campuses played a video, with Leah saying, in a whisper, "Thank you for praying."

"To have fellowship with other Christians is to enter fellowship with the Father. To have fellowship with the Father is to have fellowship with those for whom Christ died. It is to be part of God's family," wrote James Montgomery Boice (1938–2000), longtime pastor of the historic Tenth Avenue Presbyterian Church in Philadelphia.

Abby and Peter were overwhelmed with visitors in the hospital. Sara Gill remembered, "Abby was saying [to visitors from church], 'I don't know you.' She looked at me, she knew me, and we held hands.

"We have a level of comfort [with the Hansens] that you have with cousins," said Sara. Before Timmy was born, when Abby was still teaching, Sara watched the infant Leah four days a week. They called it Gillycare.

Her son Luke is three months younger than Leah. "They were each other's first playmates. Leah would give me a tough time at naps. She didn't want to sleep. She wanted to party all day. She was always very positive, ready to go. She always wanted to know what the plan was. I'm sure she could give her mother a hard time," said Sara.

Following her spinal cord stroke, Leah maintained her spunk. "She walks into a room and doesn't think what people will think of her limitations. She'll say, 'I'll try to do that.' I love that she's not self-conscious," said Sara.

Sara, who was raised in a Christian home and graduated from Liberty University, said Leah gave her a wonderful point of conversation, once people learned that she knew the eight-year-old girl who had suffered the spinal cord stroke, whose story made Page One of *The Courier-News*. "For me to talk openly about the Gospel, I used Leah. Since that moment, I had no fear of talking about Jesus with moms in my school, my neighborhood. I just talk about what the Lord did for Leah and her family, how He sent the right people at the right time. I was initially shaken [by Leah's illness] but in the long term was strengthened."

Sara remembered the milestone day when she walked into Leah's hospital room after Leah had her breathing tube removed. "She said, 'Hi, Aunt Sara.' She was sitting up. It was nice to see her smile. Her hair looked good. She had color in her face."

Another milestone was the day when the staff at Children's Specialized Hospital in New Brunswick determined the flu season had passed and children could visit Leah on the floor. "Luke was so excited he could go see her. When I was allowed to bring him, she and Luke picked up where they left off. She gave him a tour of the hospital.

"He was so nervous before we got to the hospital. When he got in the car to go home, he was so relaxed. 'I'm glad she's OK.' He's so grown-up. He has empathy."

One of the blessings, said Sara, was the support Abby and Peter had from their family and their church family. "[Abby] has three other children. God gave her strength to worry just about Leah. She could give one hundred percent to Leah. She knew everybody else could take care of the other three."

Nearly one year after Leah got sick, Liquid Church had a praise and prayer meeting. Unlike that first Wednesday night during the week Leah suffered the stroke, this time there was a celebration. In the book *Liquid Church,* which Tim Lucas coauthored with Warren Bird, he wrote, "Leah walked across the stage of our broadcast campus and our church family nearly ripped the roof off cheering and praising Jesus for his mercy and goodness. That's the power of story. And the story of a powerful God."

CHAPTER 12

Liquid

Central New Jersey played a significant role in the history of the Christian church in America. In the 1720s, Theodorus Frelinghuysen and Gilbert Tennent preached what today would be called fire-and-brimstone sermons, warning their congregations of the consequences of a life of sin, helping spur the growth of what historians call the Great Awakening.

The sons of Frelinghuysen, a Dutch Reformed preacher, helped begat Queens College in New Brunswick, now known as Rutgers University. Tennent, a Presbyterian minister, helped begat the Log College in Pennsylvania, which evolved into the College of New Jersey in Elizabeth, before it relocated in Princeton and became Princeton University. (Together, Rutgers and Princeton begat college football in 1869, for what that's worth.)

Jump to 1999. Dr. Peter Pendell, pastor of the historic Millington Baptist Church in Central New Jersey, was concerned about a yawning gap in the congregation. Children would be raised in the church, join the youth group, go off to college, and then not return to church until they had children of their own. There was no ministry for twenty-something singles—a growing demographic in our society, as many young people often put off marriage and children until their late twenties and beyond. Within that demographic was Dr. Pendell's daughter Aimee, then single. "I think he started a Sunday school class for me," she said.

What began as a Sunday school class in the church basement taught by Tim Lucas grew to become one of the largest congregations in the Northeast, with a vision to "saturate the state." Pastor Tim calls it "an accidental church plant."

In the foreword to *Liquid Church*, the book Lucas coauthored with Warren Bird, Carey Nieuwhof wrote, "This is a book about a church in New Jersey that's crushing it with thousands of unchurched people—specifically, millennials, Gen Z'ers and young families. Did you catch that? *Jersey.*

"Not to insult New Jersey, but if you were sitting in a boardroom praying and strategizing about where to plant a church that's going to saturate its state with the Gospel and reach the next generation for Christ, the guy who raises his hand and suggests Parsippany, New Jersey, is probably not going to get invited back to the next meeting."

Go right ahead, Mister Carey Nieuwhof. We can take it. Disrespect Jersey all you want. We can take a punch. I love it.

When he had that vision for a Sunday school class, Dr. Pendell approached Lucas, then an English teacher at nearby Summit High School, thinking he would be the best teacher for the class. He had grown up in the church, wearing a jacket and tie, listening to three-point sermons, and singing the first, second, and fourth stanzas of traditional hymns. The Frozen Chosen, he called it. "It was intellectually precise but relationally sterile," he said.

Lucas went to Wheaton College in Illinois, often described as the Christian Harvard, made famous by alumnus Billy Graham, and a museum that includes the actual wardrobe that inspired C. S. Lewis's *The Lion, the Witch, and the Wardrobe.* There, Tim met his wife, the former Colleen McCabe, and when she invited him to her home church, it was as if he was in a foreign land. Her church was a Pentecostal congregation that met in a Bronx storefront. A happy clappy church, he called it.

Early in their marriage, they commuted from their home in New Jersey to Manhattan, to attend Redeemer Presbyterian Church and sit under the ministry of Pastor Timothy Keller. Keller, one of the most influential Christian leaders of the twenty-first century, attracted a robust number of young people, and he became a *New York Times* go-to guy when they sought out an evangelical Christian point of view.

Tim and Colleen later moved their church home to the Millington Baptist Church, an historic 150-year-old church. They were now back in a jacket-and-tie congregation when Dr. Pendell floated the idea of beginning a Sunday morning singles' ministry in the basement. Tim famously had one question: "What time do we have to be here?"

"Nine thirty."

"OK."

From the first dozen, the class grew. The best advertisement was word of mouth. When the sessions outgrew the basement, Dr. Pendell went down the street and asked owners of the historic King George Inn if the young singles' class could meet Sunday mornings in the ballroom. Taverns are typically unused on Sunday mornings, and they rented the space.

When the ministry outgrew the tavern, Dr. Pendell asked Tim in the summer of 2001 if he would be willing to leave his job as an English teacher, join the staff at Millington Baptist, and take over the Sunday-evening service. He quit his job and joined the staff.

A few months later, the terrorist attacks of September 11,

2001, occurred. At a time when many millennials were doing an inventory of their spiritual lives, Liquid Church was now meeting in a church sanctuary and growing.

As Liquid Church grew, some members of the historic Baptist congregation were uneasy with the nontraditional meeting Sunday nights in their sanctuary. When the lights were turned low, the worship team wore faded jeans, and candles were used. Some people came to Liquid Church on motorcycles and discarded their cigarette butts in the parking lot.

"Our church sends missionaries across the ocean," Dr. Pendell told the congregation. "But we have an unreached tribe right across the street [in Central New Jersey]. To reach them, we need to speak their language, sing their style of music, and dress like part of their culture. Liquid doesn't need our criticism; it needs our celebration and support."

Resistance eased somewhat when Tim was asked to preach at a traditional Sunday-morning worship service. "It was so Bible centered no one could complain," said Dr. Pendell, a mentor to Tim, who serves on the Liquid Church board of directors. Tim calls him "The Godfather" of Liquid Church.

Abby and Peter met at Liquid Church in 2004. Not that I could have stopped her, but I would have discouraged my daughter from attending if Liquid were not Bible centered. Though she was in her midtwenties, she was still our child, and we wanted her taught well. In the Old Testament, God instructed Moses, "Assemble the people before me to hear my words so that they may learn to revere me as long as they live in the land and may teach them to their children" (Deuteronomy 4:10).

Yes, I am old. I do miss the blue hymnals. *The Old Rugged Cross. There's Power in the Blood.* I miss the rustling of Bibles when references are made to obscure verses from Habakkuk.

Today the verses are flashed on the jumbo screen and appear immediately on your Bible app.

"The old analog world was word-based, but our digital world is image-driven. The first instinct of many young adults is to communicate through texts, emojis, photos, videos, and social media," Lucas wrote in the book he coauthored with Bird.

During the glory days of newspaper journalism, New York City subway riders would bury their face in the *Daily News*. The last time I was on a commuter train, I counted sixteen passengers. Fifteen were on their smartphones. "People today have the attention span of a bumblebee," says Lucas.

The campuses of Liquid Church have their own musical team, campus leader, and small groups. The Sunday sermon is delivered to all campuses on a large video screen, sent from the broadcast center in Parsippany. It takes someone from my generation a few minutes to get used to a live streamed video preacher preaching. It takes the bumblebees nothing flat.

By 2006, the year Abby and Peter were married in a traditional tuxedo-and-wedding-gown ceremony in the Millington sanctuary, the decision was made for Liquid Church to leave Millington and find a venue of its own for Sunday-morning services. "We were very happy to be launching a baby church," said Dr. Pendell. The choice was the Hyatt Regency ballroom in Morristown, about twelve interstate miles north of Millington.

The move was an immediate success, and when Sunday-morning attendance reached about a thousand, a second campus was launched at the Hyatt Hotel in New Brunswick, adjacent to the Rutgers University campus, less than one mile from the Frelinghuysen dormitory. Abby and Peter migrated to the New Brunswick campus.

There was a time when our son Andrew's church was

meeting in a gymnasium in Boston. The church Donna and I were attending was meeting in a gymnasium in Piscataway. Our daughter Carrie was attending a church that met at a building that included a Days Inn and a Hooters restaurant in East Brunswick. Now, Abby was meeting in a hotel. (It is a family tradition. Growing up, we were part of a church plant in Union that began meeting at the American Legion Hall on Sunday mornings, only after our young pastor, Hap Arnold, arrived at sunrise to discard empty Pabst Blue Ribbon beer bottles left over from Saturday-night parties.)

These churches, in gyms and hotels, taught the faith of our fathers. There are no wooden pews, hymn books, or people dressed in their Sunday best. The gymnasium and hotel churches were preaching the Gospel of Jesus Christ and adhering to the foundation built by the first-century apostles who often met in secret, out of the view of Roman thugs whose only god was Caesar.

A consequential event in the history of the church was at a staff meeting when Warren Bird asked if any church had approached Liquid about a possible merger. "I quickly said no, caught off guard by the question," said Lucas.

"Someone will," said Bird, who gave Tim a copy of a book he'd just written, *Better Together: Making Church Mergers Work*. Tim, who had never considered the concept, added the book that night to a pile of about fifteen books he intended to read.

At six thirty the next morning—*the next morning*—Mike Leahy, who joined the staff in 2006 and became the director of campus ministries, got a phone call from an elder at the Mountainside Gospel Chapel who was related to Mike by marriage. He called with what he described as "a shot in the dark." He asked Mike, "Would you guys be open to exploring the possibility of our church becoming a campus of Liquid Church?"

Mike was amazed at the timing, considering what had been discussed less than twelve hours earlier. When Mike told Tim about the phone call, he scrambled to read Warren Bird's book.

The Mountainside church began in 1821 as a Sunday school for children, not unlike Liquid Church beginning in 1999 as a Sunday school for young singles. It reached peak attendance in the 1970s and 1980s before a slow decline. "The culture changed, but we didn't. We were more concerned with preserving the past than forging the future," said Dr. Gregg Hagg, its senior pastor. "The world around us shifted, and the ministry ossified beneath our feet."

"We spent months trying to figure out what color to paint the walls," Gregg's wife, Linda, remembered. "It was exhausting."

I had gotten to know Dr. Hagg in the 1990s when he taught a course in Newark on the life of Christ. He had studied at Dallas Theological Seminary and earned graduate degrees in Hebrew and Judaic studies at New York University, telling stories in that Newark classroom of Jesus's public ministry as they would have been better understood by first-century Jews. He would not have endorsed the merger had he not been confident in the traditional orthodox teachings of Liquid Church. His endorsement worked for me.

Finances at the Mountainside church had put it in a precarious position. When Dr. Hagg sought independent advice about mergers, he said he was told, "They don't work. Both of them were struggling, and they die together." However, Liquid Church was not struggling.

Dr. Hagg's son Andy had gone to Liquid before he moved to Texas, back when it was meeting in the tavern. "He was there the night they named Liquid Church Liquid Church. Andy was very positive about Tim, and that helped me a lot."

The Mountainside congregation voted to give the building to Liquid Church in what is known as the Miracle of Mountainside. Stained glass windows were replaced by flat-screen monitors. Pews were removed, and as Dr. Hagg explained it, "The decibels of the music were raised."

A total of about a thousand people attended four services held that first Sunday. Then the congregation at the 121-year-old United Church of Christ in Garwood, after learning the Mountainside story, voted to dissolve and donate its building to Liquid. This would be known as the Gift of Garwood.

With equity in properties in Mountainside and Garwood, Liquid Church was then able to obtain a mortgage on the 165,000-square-foot office and warehouse building in Parsippany, near the intersection of Interstates 287 and 80. There Liquid Church built its broadcast center, church offices, and a worship center. "I never dreamed what Liquid became. Never," said Dr. Pendell. "It's been a fun adventure to be part of."

Abby and Peter would be part of several migrations, moving their church home from Millington to Morristown to New Brunswick to Mountainside. Then a campus was begun in Somerset County, and Abby and Peter and a bloc of their close friends began attending the Liquid Church at Somerville Middle School. When the COVID-19 pandemic was easing, they began attending the Parsippany campus.

Prior to the pandemic, Preakness Faith Community Church in Wayne donated its property and a 12,000-square-foot building to Liquid Church. In June 2021, Princeton Meadow Church donated its building and more than seven acres of property to Liquid.

When that merger with Mountainside Gospel Chapel was

taking place, Tim remembered asking a man who had been a longtime member of the congregation what he thought of the plan. He told Tim, "We're not big fans of your music. It's too loud. I wear earplugs when I visit." (At the main campus in Parsippany complimentary earplugs are available.)

So, then Tim asked why he voted to approve the merger. With tears in his eyes, he said, "Because you're baptizing our grandchildren."

This is our story too.

In the summer of 2019, Leah and Timmy were baptized in the Atlantic Ocean by Somerville campus pastor Jon Coords, after about four thousand people had attended a Sunday-morning worship service Liquid Church hosted at the historic Great Auditorium in Ocean Grove.

The roster of Liquid Church members who helped Leah would be a long one.

In 2004, Keri Dolbier, a member of the congregation since its beginning, helped organize HisKids to produce a Christmas drama and musical program that began rehearsals in early September and put on its program in December at Millington Baptist Church. In 2017, Leah was a ballerina in a production called *We Three Spies*.

When Leah was hospitalized in March 2018, Keri was one of scores of visitors to her room in the PICU. "I was so impressed with her parents. 'Leah, you're going to get better.' She was just a child, and children bounce back quickly."

Six months after the spinal cord stroke, Leah tried out for a singing part for the HisKids 2018 program, *I Heard the Bells on Christmas Day*. Keri did not rig the tryout to make certain Leah was chosen. "I remember thinking, *I sure hope she can sing.* But Leah earned the part and blended right in, with a solo."

Keri said that observing the progress Leah made did far

more than strengthen her faith. "It reaffirmed it," she said. "All these small miracles we've seen—we give God all the glory. He has taken the worst thing and made it a beautiful thing."

Before Leah's hospitalization, Abby and Peter and the kids were part of a small group hosted by Tim and Maria Scholma, at their home in Hillsborough. During Leah's hospitalization, the elder Hansens would bring the twins to the Somerville campus, and we would bring Timmy. Following cleanup after the 11:00 a.m. service, the Scholmas brought all three to their home, putting them in a familiar environment while giving the grandparents an afternoon of rest. We nominated the Scholmas for sainthood.

The Liquid Church golden moment would be when a team of men from the congregation resurrected a tree.

CHAPTER 13

Praying for a Tree

When Leah was born, Peter marked her birth by planting a cherry tree in the front yard. He later planted trees for Timmy, Serena, and Joey.

Each spring, Leah's tree explodes in a burst of pink blossoms. What the tree could not handle well in March 2018, however, was the covering of heavy wet snow that began falling during the second night of Leah's hospitalization.

Following another long and grueling day at the Morristown hospital, Peter returned home to a heartbreaking scene. The weight of the snow split Leah's tree down the middle. One half fell into the driveway. Remarkably, both halves were still connected to the root system. His eight-year-old daughter was broken. The tree was broken. Peter was broken. But he was convinced that in the hands of specialists, the tree could recover. "The tree was not going to die, because Leah was not going to die," he determined.

Peter is handy, and under normal circumstances, would have tried to repair the tree, but he could not so when he was spending eighteen hours a day at Leah's bedside. He called Ryan Smerillo, a skilled carpenter by trade. "I said, 'Ryan, you gotta do something.'"

Ryan, a member of Liquid Church known as Uncle Ryan to the Hansen kids, took the call while driving his pickup. "Peter was in a state of emotion I never heard before. He was trying to gather his words to explain what had happened."

Ryan and his wife, Kristin, knew Leah from the day she was born. (It was Kristin who directed the bridal parties during Abby and Peter's wedding ceremony.) The Smerillos understood the significance of the tree, and Ryan remembered thinking, "It was time to rally the troops. The first call I made was to Jeff Allen."

Jeff Allen is a licensed landscape architect who grew up near woods in northern Vermont, about fifteen miles south of the Canadian border. He would create a plan to save the tree, and he and Ryan put together a team that would include Drew Huber, Josh Gill, and Tim Scholma.

Jeff purchased threaded rods, washers, bolts, a drill bit, and tie-down ratchet straps. The team gathered at the tree, lifted the two halves, and used three rods and the straps to secure them.

The team surrounded the tree and prayed. "I never prayed for a tree before," said Jeff. "We prayed for the tree, we prayed for Peter and Abby, we prayed for Leah. It was simultaneously silly—to be praying for a tree to live—and spiritual. I remember it being so sad, looking at the dark and vacant house, knowing why it was dark and vacant."

Though the rods and bolts seemed to achieve a tight fit, Jeff was concerned that moisture or bugs might penetrate the tiniest of gaps and cause rot from inside the tree.

In a text message to Peter, he said, "I researched and consulted with some CTEs [certified tree experts] and the best sealant is beeswax. Flexible and natural. So, I bought a couple of pounds and will melt it into the wound."

Peter replied in a text: "You take your tree work seriously!

Thank you So, So much. That tree is going to not only survive, but it will also thrive! As will Leah!"

Jeff responded, "I normally don't care this much about one tree, but this is Leah we're talking about."

Several nights later, when there was a forecast for more snow, Jeff went alone at about nine o'clock, borrowed a ladder from Peter's shed, and pruned the tree to lessen the weight that might compromise the repair.

Jeff is married to the former Jan Cerrigione, who we met earlier. It was she who approached Peter fourteen years earlier at a rest stop on the New York Thruway when a group from Liquid Church, including Abby, was going on a ski trip. "You're going to be our friend," Jan told him. The rest is history: Peter would marry Abby. Jeff would marry Jan. And a tree would flourish.

CHAPTER 14

Ye Must Be Born Again

The principal job of a Christian church is not about putting on musicals or restoring broken trees. It is to bring people into the family of believers in Jesus Christ and prepare the family to enjoy God forever.

On the sixth day in the pediatric intensive care unit at the Morristown hospital, the most perilous part of Leah's hospitalization seemed to be over, now that she could move her right toes and her breathing was under control.

Then Abby and Peter realized they were not 100 percent certain Leah had ever asked Jesus into her heart. Surely Leah had heard the children's version of the salvation story, but had she ever asked Jesus into her heart, to be her savior?

At 11:52 p.m., Peter wrote, "Tonight Abby and I talked with sweet Leah about what it means to ask Jesus into your heart, and then we prayed. When we finished praying, I asked her if she had prayed along with me. She gave me a quick blink of her eyes, her new signal for 'Yes.' (Nodding is difficult so we found a better system. 'No' is a *long* blink.)

"So at about 11:30 p.m. in a dark hospital room, Jesus heard the silent prayer of a largely paralyzed eight-year-old girl who can't speak, and He entered into her heart. There are many angels singing tonight!"

Peter added, "God placed it on my heart that we are doing a lot of praying *for* Leah, but God wants Leah to pray for *herself.* And now Leah is first in the line of God's children begging Him to restore her."

Jesus said, "Let the little children come to me, and do not hinder them, for the kingdom of heaven belongs to such as these" (Matthew 19:14).

On that night when Leah blinked rapidly, what exactly happened? Is that all you need to do to become a born-again Christian? *Blink?* And what does "born again" even mean?

When a member of the Jewish ruling council named Nicodemus was told by Jesus that he needed to be born again, Nicodemus said, "Surely he cannot enter a second time into his mother's womb" (John 3:4). He likely said it with a snarky tone.

No one ever decided when and where to be born the natural way. No one chose their parents, or the time and place, or whether they would have blue eyes or brown. We all were born once the old-fashioned way.

When a person is "born again," the Bible teaches, he or she is "born from above." We once were dead in our sins, and when the Bible says dead, it means dead. As a doornail. Lifeless. The dead cannot rouse themselves. They must be roused if they are to have a new life.

"All is of God," wrote Archbishop William Temple (1881–1944). "The only thing of my very own which I contribute to my redemption is the sin from which I need to be redeemed." A version of that quote has also been attributed to Martin Luther's contemporary Philip Melanchthon and Jonathan Edwards, and it could be said of all believers.

Few brought more sin to the equation than John Newton

(1725–1807), once the captain of a slave ship, who had a born-again experience and wrote the hymn "Amazing Grace." God found him and, Newton wrote, "saved a wretch like me." The bar to salvation cannot reach much higher than an eighteenth-century slave trader, but we all fell short of God's expectations, and only faith in Jesus will save us.

In his biography of Ligonier Ministry founder R.C. Sproul, author Stephen Nichols described the focus of Sproul's ministry: "1. God is holy. 2. We are not. 3. We need a substitute. These three propositions came to serve as the foundation for his teaching."

Writing in *The Cross. God's Way of Salvation,* English preacher Dr. David Martyn Lloyd-Jones explained that Jesus died on the cross because He loved us. "The cross tells me that I am a complete failure, and that I am such a failure that he had to come from heaven, not merely to teach and preach in this world, but to die on that cross. Nothing else could save us."

It is the work of the Holy Spirit. "We do not give birth to ourselves. We are not reborn because we believe. We believe because we are reborn," wrote Dr. Lloyd-Jones.

A most difficult concept to understand is the belief that God elected to have believers join his kingdom "before the world began."

The election of believers mirrors God's selection of the Jews, as described in the Hebrew Bible. After the Israelites crossed the Red Sea, and before entering their promised land, Moses told them, "The Lord your God had chosen you out of all the peoples on the face of the earth to be His people, His treasured possession" (Deuteronomy 7:8).

To this day, we refer to Jews as the chosen people. One sign of the authenticity of the Bible is the way the tribe of Israelites has survived as a people group. There were scores of tribes in Bible times—Canaanites, Hittites, Amorites, Perizzites, Hivites, Jebusites. They have been absorbed into other cultures. The Hebrew tribe survived slavery in Egypt, the Babylonian captivity, first-century persecution, the Inquisition, and the Holocaust. Today, Jerusalem remains a focus of world geopolitics, and antisemitism is real.

In 2008, I traveled to Israel with the Jewish Federation of Greater Middlesex County. We visited the old city hall in Tel Aviv where David Ben Gurion announced the birth of the modern state of Israel on May 14, 1948. (The only section of Tel Aviv that Christian tour groups typically visit is the modern airport.) In the foyer of the old city hall are Bible verses from the books of Jeremiah, Isaiah, and Amos. The verses in Amos declare, "'I will bring back my exiled people Israel; they will rebuild the ruined cities and live in them. They will plant vineyards and drink their wine; they will make gardens and eat their fruit. I will plant Israel in their own land, never to be uprooted from the land I have given them,' says the Lord your God" (Amos 9:14–15). The prophet Amos wrote those words about 750 years before the birth of Christ, about 2,700 years before Ben Gurion's announcement. When God chooses a people, He chooses for keeps.

Some people have great stories about making a "decision for Christ." Once they were rebellious teenagers, swindlers, drunks, or deadbeat dads. Charles Colson was President Richard M. Nixon's "hatchet man," caught up in the Watergate scandal. He went to prison, and there Jesus found him. Colson told his story in a book he called *Born Again*.

In 1976, soon after we moved, I registered in time to vote for Jimmy Carter in the Democratic Party's June primary, rewarding him for being so open about being "born again." Around that same time, tennis player Bjorn Borg was winning numerous major titles, and headline writers could not resist: "Bjorn Again."

However, you do not become a born-again Christian by merely blinking your eyes in a hospital bed when prompted by your parents. Nor do you become a Christian by raising your hand at the end of a compelling sermon or walking the aisle at a Billy Graham Crusade. We're not saved by going through the motions.

In 2014, our son Andrew married Elizabeth Jemison at her home church in Memphis. Leah, then five, was the flower girl, and Timmy, then four, was the ring bearer. Both did perfect jobs. After the service, an excited Timmy said to me, "I got married today! I walked up the aisle!"

Well, yes and no. He walked up the aisle—and we have the adorable pictures to prove it. But he did not get married. He just went through the motions.

The way I tell my salvation story is that I made a public profession of faith when Billy Graham spoke at the Great Auditorium in Ocean Grove on August 26, 1956. Like Leah in that hospital room, I was eight years old. It seemed to come naturally. My parents were Christians; my grandparents, my aunts and uncles, and my cousins were Christians. I began going to church nine months before I was born. Wasn't I a Christian all along?

Salvation by genealogy? That's not how it works.

"Just because I'm Billy Graham's daughter doesn't mean I'm a child of God," said Anne Graham Lotz. "I had to make that decision for myself, on my own."

Jonathan Schaeffer was pastor of our church in Piscataway before leaving in 1998 to lead the congregation of Grace Church in Middleburg, Ohio. In a series of sermons from the book of Romans, he explained how other religions base salvation on good works, obedience to rituals, or perhaps a pilgrimage. "You develop your résumé spiritually and you present it to God. If it's my résumé I'm done. I'm sunk. What [the New Testament book of] Romans teaches is you get a résumé from above. It's not how good you can be for God. It's about how good God has been to you."

The concept of being chosen by God before the world was made is not a consensus belief among professing Christians. Every two years, Ligonier Ministry and Lifeway Research conduct a theological survey. Researchers made the following statement: "God chose people he would save before he created the world."

Thirty-nine percent of respondents who identify as "evangelical" either strongly believed or somewhat believed that statement. But 44 percent, a plurality, either strongly disagreed or somewhat disagreed.

While I belong in the column that says we were chosen before the foundation of the world, I also believe we can decide to be one of those chosen before the foundation, which seems like I have just twisted the pretzel. If the Holy Spirit plants the desire, and you ask God to take away your sin because of the sacrifice of Jesus Christ on the God will accept you into His family, here and now.

It is complicated, in part, because we do not understand God's dimension of time.

"Before the foundation of the world" is, in His dimension, as much as today and tomorrow and eternity past and present. "With the blessed Holy Spirit there is no yesterday or tomorrow— there is only an everlasting now. And since he is altogether God, enjoying the attributes of the Godhead, there is with Him no elsewhere," wrote A.W. Tozer. "He inhabits an eternal here. His center is everywhere. His boundary is nowhere."

God is not bound by our dimension of time. "Time is nature's way of keeping everything from happening at once"—a quote attributed to Mark Twain, Albert Einstein, and science fiction writer Ray Cummings, among others.

Historians refer to the "passage of time." Everything created in our world is becoming what it is not. Mount Everest has been changed by the wind over the past twenty-four hours. We are not today what we were yesterday or will be tomorrow. But God—the great I AM—does not have a growth chart. Billy Graham wrote, While our world is shaking and crumbling, we need to realize that one thing will never change, and that is God. He is the same today as He was ten million years ago, and He will be the same ten million years from today. We are like grasshoppers; we appear and hop around a bit on the earth, and then we are gone."

Francis T. Collins, author of *The Language of God*, wrote, "If God exists then He is supernatural. If He is supernatural, then He is not limited by natural laws. If he is not limited by natural laws, there is no reason He should be limited by time. If He is not limited by time, then He is in the past, present and future."

August 26, 1956, was the night I walked the aisle when Billy Graham spoke in Ocean Grove. But that date is how we measure time. "For he chose us in him before the creation of the world to be holy and blameless in his sight. In love he predestined us to be adopted as sons [and daughters] through Jesus Christ, in accordance to His pleasure and will" (Ephesians 1: 4–5).

If God inhabits "the everlasting now," the events of August 26, 1956, were occurring before creation of the world. So when was Leah born again? The night of March 11, 2018, and before the creation of the world.

CHAPTER 15

Adoption into the Family

Leah, her parents, and grandparents—and Anne Graham Lotz—were not born into God's family. The New Testament book of Ephesians tells us we were *adopted*. Adoption, as we know it in our culture, is a beautiful way to illustrate the family of believers.

Ann Hansen is not sure who was speaking one summer at Camp of The Woods in Upstate New York, or exactly what was said, but something planted the idea with her that she and Art should adopt a child. Ann remembers walking down to the lake with Peter and his sisters' Deborah and Elizabeth to tell the kids what she and Art were thinking. Elizabeth would be too young to understand what they were saying, but Deborah and Peter did. "What are you doing?" they said. Mom and Dad were in their fifties, and they wanted *another* kid? Really?

They sought out an agency in Russia, and the way Art explains it, the paperwork was staggering. Think income tax return times ten. (This was in 2001. Beginning January 1, 2013, the Russian government banned adoptions by US citizens.)

The process was never smooth. They had been given the profile of a young girl, and twice the process was halted when Russian families jumped the line. If a Russian family wanted the girl, their desire would trump the Americans. Both Russian families eventually balked at keeping this little girl. The Hansens were told it was because the Russian families did not "connect" with her.

Finally, the Hansens were given the OK to fly to Moscow, then take a train one thousand kilometers to the east and a five-hour car ride to the orphanage. They were accompanied by a former colonel in the Russian air force, who laid down the law. "He looked me in the eye and said, 'You must connect,'" recalled Art, mimicking the rigid command.

When they were brought to the room to meet the girl, they understood why she failed to connect with two Russian families. She had a stern look on her face that seemed to be saying, in any language, "This ain't happening.'"

Then Art slowly blew up a beach ball and played catch with Ann. They played catch with their translator and then with the girl. Ann had brought a stroller and a doll, and that helped break the ice. When the team from the orphanage left the room, Ann sealed the deal with a piece of chocolate. The next day when the girl entered a room where the Hansens were waiting, she ran to Art and hugged him. They had connected!

On August 1, 2001, several weeks before her fifth birthday, they brought the girl they named Sarah Anastasia Hansen to the United States, a day marked annually as her "fly date." She is a co-heir with Deborah, Peter, and Elizabeth.

All Christians have been adopted. "Yet to all who receive him, to those who believed in his name, he gave the right to be children of God—children born not of natural descent, nor of human decision or a husband's will, but born of God" (John 1:12–13).

"Now if we are children, then we are heirs—heirs of God and co-heirs with Christ, if indeed we share in his sufferings in order that we may also share in his glory" (Romans 8:17).

CHAPTER 16

Ye Must Persevere

The testimonies of people like Charles Colson, John Newton, and the eight-year-old girl who blinked in her hospital bed are great stories. But we are not saved by testimony. The profession of faith is only the start of a race.

The walk-the-aisle invitation at Billy Graham Crusades was first used by Charles Finney in the 1800s and popularized by Billy Sunday and Dwight Moody in the twentieth century. It became known as an "altar call."

But by itself, walking an aisle and kneeling at an altar does not make one a Christian.

In a sermon preached at Parkside Church in Cleveland on January 26, 1997, Alistair Begg said, "You see, people say to me, 'Well, why don't you have an altar call every Sunday? And why don't we have the drama of everybody, you know, putting up their hands, and walking down aisles, and doing all those things?' Well, there's a variety of reasons for that, but one is this: That of all the people who walk those aisles, and put up their hands, and sign the cards, and do all those things, the percentage return of continuance along the journey is so, so dreadfully low. I delight to see my children walking in the truth. For it is as we walk in the truth, as we continue to the end, as we keep our eyes fixed on the goal, that we give testimony to the fact that we are truly in Christ."

In "The Fruitless Vine," a sermon preached by Charles Haddon Spurgeon at Park Street Chapel in London on April 22, 1857, he said, "I do tremble for many young people in my church—I will not exclude my own church. They get an idea into their heads that they are converted: The work was not true, not genuine, not real; it was an excitement; it was a stir in the conscience for a while, and it will not last.

"Many have thought themselves converted when they were not; hundreds of thousands have had an impression, a kind of conversion, not real, which for a while endured, but afterward it passed away as summer's dream."

Spurgeon added, "Oh! Thou who art valiant for truth, thou wouldst have been as valiant for the devil if grace had not laid hold of thee. A seat in heaven shall one day be thine; but a chain in hell would have been thine if grace had not changed thee."

A familiar Old Testament story illustrates the need to persevere, from the time one walks an aisle, raises his hand, or blinks her eyes. Moses reminded the Israelites, "The Lord took you and brought you out of the iron-smelting furnace, out of Egypt, to be the people of his inheritance" (Deuteronomy 4:20). This was a picture of the conversion experience. The Hebrews walked the aisle, through the Red Sea, saved from the devil at their heels.

Moses later told them, "Remember how the Lord your God led you all the way in the desert these 40 years, to humble you and to test you, in order to know what was in your heart, whether or not you would keep his commands" (Deuteronomy 8:2). Instead of the word *test*, as it appears in the New International Version, the King James Version uses the word *prove*. You say you are a Christian; prove it.

"The only validation you will ever have of your salvation is a life of obedience. It is the only possible proof that you recognize the Lordship of Jesus Christ," said John MacArthur, pastor of Grace Community Church in Sun Valley, California. "It's not as simple as signing a card, raising your hand. Salvation is a recognition of the divine standard, a subsequent overwhelming sense of sinfulness, a pleading for God's mercy to receive His righteousness because you desire to fulfill His Word."

I write this more than four years out from the night Leah blinked her eyes, saying she understood the message of Jesus Christ and accepted it. Her life since then has been fruitful. Her story had changed people. She is *proving* her faith.

The woman who headed the loan division at the bank where we got our mortgage explained that when the bank grants a homeowner a thirty-year mortgage, the bank wants to be certain the buyer can make payments from start to finish. "We know you can make the first few payments," I recall her saying. "We want to know if you can make the three hundred and sixtieth payment."

R.C. Sproul told the story about his conversion experience, when he and best friend, Johnny, who were attending college together in the Pittsburgh area, made a profession of faith on a Friday. Before they went to bed that night, they wrote their girlfriends to tell them about their conversions. The next morning, according to biographer Stephen Nichols, Sproul was eager to talk with his friend about what happened the night before. "He didn't want to talk about it. He just rolled over like it never happened. All Johnny wanted to do was to make it to Youngstown that night. But R.C. truly had been turned from his sin and was turned toward God." Sproul (1939-2017) founded Ligonier Ministries in 1971 in Western Pennsylvania, a ministry I have leaned on heavily.

The apostle Paul speaks of those who "wander from the faith." The author of the book of Hebrews warns about "drifting away." Even the most devout Christians are prone to drift. We all have our own version of the prodigal son story. Our story will end well when we return to the Father.

I was blessed with wonderful role models of men who persevered. Abby's maternal grandfather, Roger Johnson, became an ordained Baptist minister in his seventies. My father was active in his church in his late eighties. Abby's grandmothers were pillars in their church. So were Peter's grandparents. My brother Nelson was retired when he founded an international ministry. There have been many men who served as role models and persevered: my father, my uncle Eddie, my brothers Nelson and Dan, and my three children's fathers-in-law, Art Hansen, Frank Jemison, and Bill Walker.

No one in my Christian experience finished better than Jim McDonald, who headed a ministry known as Meeting God in Missions. I went on six mission trips with him to the Dominican Republic. Most of the trips involved building projects for Haitian congregations whose men worked the sugarcane fields. (On my most recent trip my job was to hold a flashlight while a dental student from Santo Domingo extracted teeth.)

Jim was born in 1938, raised in poverty in Appalachia, and abandoned by his abusive father when he was ten. He earned a basketball scholarship to West Virginia Wesleyan University and was selected by the Cincinnati Royals in the 1962 National Basketball Association draft. Jim became a successful college basketball coach, leading the US team to a gold medal at an international tournament in Israel in 1976.

His Christian life began when he made a public profession of faith at the age of twelve. He figured he then went more than forty years without ever reading a single chapter in the Bible. He said the only verses he knew were John 3:16 and "Jesus wept."

He was reawakened when he and his sixteen-year-old son stumbled upon Charles Stanley, an Atlanta pastor, preaching on television. Soon, upward of twenty-five people were in his home on Friday nights, discussing what they saw on Stanley's *In Touch Ministry* broadcasts. Then, in 1994, he went on a mission trip led by a Christian and Missionary Alliance congregation in Erie, Pennsylvania.

Looking back at the trajectory of his life, he recalled his triumphs as a basketball player and coach. "Then I see myself many years later standing in a sugar cane village, holding a little Haitian girl in my arms. The snot is running from her nose onto my shirt as she clasps my arms and it dawns on me—this is better than the gold medal I won in Israel. God didn't create me for sports," he wrote in his autobiography, *A Journey with God*.

"Hundreds of those who have journeyed with God in Haiti and the DR have gone back home changed. They're serving God as never before in their family situation, in their local churches and in their communities, and their lives will never be the same," wrote McDonald, who died in December 2020. He had run the race. Well done, Jim McDonald.

The year I retired from the newspaper, I rode my bicycle in the Tour de Farms, a charity event to provide support for people with multiple sclerosis. What especially appealed to me was that the event was held in flat farm country, beginning and ending at the University of Northern Illinois in DeKalb. The start was easy; the finish required perseverance.

I set out on a fifty-mile course, but in the middle of the event, I got ambitious, adding a loop that would make the distance sixty-one miles. About ten miles from the finish line, I could see the top of the twelve-story Grant Towers on the UNI campus. Readers of *The Pilgrim's Progress* would recognize the dorms as my Celestial City. What helped were those on the side of the road cheering us to the end, a modest cloud of witnesses.

About one hundred yards from the finish line, a woman and her children cheered on "Grandpa!" Their grandpa. I took that to mean me too. I finished and got a medal. (If I had not persevered and quit in the middle, do you think I would be telling you this story?)

"Great is the art of beginning," wrote poet Henry Wadsworth Longfellow, "but greater the art is of ending."

CHAPTER 17

20:43

So Leah's Baba Rick rode his bike sixty-one miles on a flat course with unlimited breaks, and at times he coasted. What does he want, a medal? (Uh, yeah.)

On October 6, 2021, Leah Hansen, running with the Long Hill Central School cross-country team, covered the course at Summit High School in 20:43. Two weeks earlier, she ran the same course in 24:28. Abby gave partial credit for the improved time to Sarah Hansen, for her attendance at the meet—three years after Leah took her first steps across her hospital room, showing off for Sarah.

In that second race in Summit, she finished seventy-eighth out of eighty-three. In subsequent races, she would finish closer to last place—not because she was slowing down but because girls who ran slower in earlier meets quit cross-country altogether. Leah would not quit.

"Why do some people have the perseverance and others don't?" said Coach Maura Aimette. "She perseveres. That is quintessential Leah."

Before her spinal cord stroke, Leah was game for everything: softball, basketball, soccer, field hockey, gymnastics. Skills required for cross-country are not that complicated: you want to run, you run. "She's a model for being grateful for her chance to run," said Coach Aimette. "It does not seem to bother Leah that she has limitations. She's impervious to that," said the coach, who was not surprised to see Leah at the first practice in September.

During the Zoom school year of 2020–21, Aimette had Leah as a sixth-grade student in her English class. What impressed her then was Leah's maturity. "Her personality is that way naturally, except she has had experiences interacting with adults that others haven't had," referring to the times Leah has told her story to a room filled with adults, during fundraising events for the Children's Miracle Network and Children's Specialized Hospital.

Philip Salerno, the president and chief development officer for the Children's Specialized Hospital Foundation, recalled how he had run cross-country in high school and college. "They don't have cuts for cross-country. You want to run, you show up and run. You are part of a team, and there is something special being on a team, something bigger than yourself."

When each cross-country meet was over, Abby typically would offer Leah a ride home. Leah instead rode on the team bus back to school, to be with her teammates, and Abby would follow and pick up Leah outside the school. "I noticed that too. Wanting to be part of a team. I like that," said Coach Aimette.

Had Leah had not suffered the spinal cord stroke and been able to run with ease, finishing, say, fifth or twenty-fifth out of eighty-three, we would have been pleased. But not the way we were thrilled when she finished seventy-eighth. The suffering she has overcome made her competing in cross-country events more meaningful.

In the spring of 2022 Leah ran track, participating in the 800-meter and the long jump. Her best in the long jump was five feet four inches—remarkable considering how she had overcome paralysis.

In the preface to *Surprised by Suffering, The Role of Pain and Death in the Christian Life,* R.C. Sproul wrote, "I want you to see that suffering is not at all uncommon, but also that is not random—it is sent by our heavenly Father, who is both sovereign and loving, for ultimate good. Indeed, I want you to understand that suffering is a vocation, a calling from God."

John Piper wrote, "For those who trust Christ, God's sovereignty is not an unyielding problem but an unfailing hope. It means that, in the suffering of Christians, neither Satan, nor man, nor nature, nor chance is wielding decisive control. God is sovereign over this suffering, which means it is not meaningless. It is purposeful. It is measured, wise and loving."

Piper added, "For every one person whom I have heard or seen forsaking the truth of God's all-pervasive providence because of suffering—or, more often because of the suffering and death of a loved one—I have seen *10* others bear witness that the biblical truth of God's absolute sovereignty, in and over their suffering and loss."

CHAPTER 18

Where Was God?

On April 18, 1995, Donna received a phone call from the chaplain at Lancaster [Pennsylvania] General Hospital. Her parents, Roger and Agnes Johnson, were in a car accident in Pennsylvania's Amish country. Donna was told that her mother, who had been disabled by a severe stroke six years earlier, died instantly. Her father was unconscious and in serious condition. When he emerged from his coma, he was transferred to a rehab facility in New Jersey, then lived briefly with us before going to his home in Livingston, where he lived for fifteen years before dying in his own bed.

The day after the car accident, Donna and I, her sister Dee Swilling, and her husband, Bill, were getting ready to go to the funeral home in Livingston to arrange for Agnes's burial, when we heard early news reports about an explosion in downtown Oklahoma City. It was soon reported that a truck had exploded in front of the Alfred P. Murrah Federal Building, and as the day wore on, the death toll kept rising. It would reach 168, including nineteen children who died at a day care center.

My cousin the Rev. Kenneth Blank—known as Butch growing up down the street from us on Vauxhall Road in Union—was then a chaplain at Presbyterian Hospital in Oklahoma City. He was in a meeting in the hospital's auditorium when the building shook. It felt like an earthquake, he said. Bits of soundproofing material fell from the ceiling like snowflakes. He thought maybe a gasoline truck had exploded outside the hospital. A colleague thought a helicopter had crashed onto the heliport.

He went to the roof and could see smoke coming from about a mile away, not far from the law office where his wife, Audrey, worked. Her office was south of the federal building. The explosion was on the north side.

Several months later, I was preparing a sermon following a tragedy in our church family. I called Butch with a simple question: where was God in Oklahoma City? He had given it a lot of thought.

Surely an all-powerful and all-loving God could have prevented the Oklahoma City bombing, just like he could have grounded the drunk driver who killed Donna's sister Joyce and the cancer that caused my sister Ginny's painful death. He could have prevented Leah's spinal cord stroke.

Butch had a four-point response.

First, he said, "God weeps. He wept with us," in Oklahoma City.

We know from the Bible that Jesus wept when he went to the house of Lazarus, who had died four days earlier. His sisters, Martha and Mary, were weeping, and they scolded Jesus for not having been there to perform a miracle and save their brother. "Jesus wept," according to John 11:35.

Jesus was not weeping over the death of Lazarus, I believe. He knew he could later say, "Lazarus, come out!" and Lazarus would walk out of the grave. He wept because Martha and Mary were weeping over another consequence of living in a fallen world, marred by sin. The Bible teaches that among the many consequences of Adam sinning in the Garden of Eden was that one day Adam would surely die, women would suffer pain in childbirth, farmers would be cursed with thorns, and millennia later, evil men would blow up a federal office building.

The second point Butch offered was that God provided an answer to sin. "For the wages of sin is death," the apostle Paul wrote in Romans 6:23. "But the gift of God is eternal life in Christ Jesus our Lord."

The third point Butch made was that God placed within many people the incentive to help when they saw human suffering. The tragedy, he said, "Brought out the good in people here [in Oklahoma City]."

People responded with good works, including area pastors who came to Presbyterian Hospital to offer support. (They all meant well, though occasionally they were off-key. "Pastors are paid to talk," Butch said. "Chaplains are paid to listen.")

We saw the community act this way after the Twin Towers fell, when Salvation Army trucks rushed to the scene and volunteers from all over the country joined the bucket brigade carrying debris from Ground Zero. We see it when towns hold clothing drives and stock food banks for victims of fire and floods, when teams of volunteers help rebuild homes damaged by hurricanes and tornadoes, when strangers pull people from burning cars.

Jeff Wanamaker, whose daughter Kathryn played softball with Leah, is a career firefighter in Millburn and an EMS volunteer in Long Hill. On September 11, 2001, he drove an engine truck to Staten Island to provide backup coverage. The next day, he went to Ground Zero and was one of hundreds of emergency personnel from around the country who volunteered to search through the rubble looking for survivors, risking their own health. (One poignant story he told was how when the remains of a firefighter were found members of the FDNY told all others to move out of the way; they insisted on taking care of one of their own.)

Jeff teaches courses on CPR, and he said he tells participants not to do mouth-to-mouth resuscitation on someone unless the person is a relative or a close friend and they know the person will not transmit a disease. "But I tell them, if someone hands you a baby who is turning blue, you're going to do mouth-to-mouth. Ninety-nine percent of you will. It's human nature." Several times, he has responded to an accident and done CPR on a stranger. "The thought to help kicks in first," he explained.

In a column that appeared in the *Wall Street Journal* twenty years after the events of September 11, 2001, Peggy Noonan recalled how 9/11 was a "deeply communal event."

She wrote, "We were all in it together, wounded together and mourning together. We dug deep, found our best selves, and actually saw the best selves in others. The spontaneous community of those who showed up at the hospital to give blood, of those on the top floors of the towers who gathered to try to lead people out, of those on the plane who banded together to storm the pilot's door—'Let's roll.' It wasn't just you, you were part of something."

In the days after 9/11, the Associated Press sent member newspapers lists of known victims. At the *Home News Tribune*, we divided assignments and went to families of those who lost their lives. Two days after the attacks, my random assignment was Todd Beamer of Cranbury, a passenger on United Flight 93, which was scheduled to fly from Newark to San Francisco. Several passengers had called relatives on the ground and learned what had happened at the World Trade Center and Pentagon. Passengers then thwarted the terrorists who were diverting the plane to Washington, and Flight 93 was crashed into an abandoned strip mine near Shanksville, Pennsylvania.

At Todd Beamer's home, I met his wife, Lisa Beamer, and their friends who attended Princeton Alliance Church in Plainsboro. Todd and Lisa were graduates of Wheaton College. Todd's friends were certain he would have joined the effort to fight the hijackers. He was the type of guy to bowl over a catcher on a play at home plate in a church softball league.

The next day, Lisa received an incident report from United Airlines about a call Todd had made from the plane to a United call center in Chicago. Todd explained how the terrorists breached the cockpit and took control of the plane. He said the Lord's Prayer with Lisa Jefferson, the woman at the call center. The last thing Lisa Jefferson heard before the call ended was, "Let's roll."

One of Todd's friends faxed me a copy of the report, and that Sunday, I, and a reporter for the *Pittsburgh Post-Gazette* with whom I was sharing information, published the exclusive story. Lisa Beamer became an important voice in the weeks to follow. Her story, *Let's Roll,* became the number one nonfiction book on the *New York Times* bestseller list.

I would interview other family members and friends of those killed on United 93, and they all told stories about how their loved one may have assisted other passengers.

Closer to home, "Leah was our 9/11," said Joe Tremarco, brother of Leah's second-grade teacher and coach of the Watchung Regional High School baseball team, referring to the generous support of Long Hill Township to the Hansen family in the spring of 2018.

The fourth part of Butch's response to events in Oklahoma City was that "God is God." God has reasons we will never understand.

Butch had a twin sister, Pat Blank Egleston. (In the neighborhood, she was known as Sis. Butch and Sis.) After graduation from Union High School, she went to college in Lock Haven, Pennsylvania, and became a career teacher. Her daughter Stephanie moved to Rhode Island, raising Pat's two granddaughters, Maddie and Julie.

Maddie Potts was seventeen. She was a popular girl who played three sports at Chariho High School in Wood River Junction, Rhode Island. During a soccer game on the night of September 24, 2017, play was stopped while Maddie prepared to take a free kick. All eyes were fixed on her—players from both teams, spectators, her thirteen-year-old sister Julie and her dad, who was filming the game to produce a video to send to college recruiters.

Suddenly, Maddie's legs buckled, and she collapsed, going into cardiac arrest. The parent of a player, a medical professional, administered CPR, and Maddie's heart resumed beating. But by then she was already brain-dead from an undiagnosed brain aneurysm. "Maddie was never sick, and as a three-sport athlete, she never had a sports injury," said my cousin Pat.

Pat's daughter Stephanie, a physician assistant, was working in the ER at a nearby hospital when she received the call about her daughter's collapse, and she immediately went to the local hospital where Maddie had first been taken. Maddie and her parents were then taken to the Hasbro Children's Hospital in Providence, where a team of medical personnel was unable to save her.

Her mom and dad were at Maddie's bedside when she was pronounced dead. Stephanie and Dan then had to tell Julie that her older sister, her hero and best friend, had died. "No all-loving God should allow a child to experience this kind of suffering," said Pat.

"The initial sense of loss, the excruciating pain and suffering slowly subsides over time, but it lies close to the surface and can return at any moment without warning," Pat told me.

Maddie's parents created the Maddie Potts Foundation. The foundation has hosted scores of events, raising money for a scholarship and to help finance the building of the Maddie Potts Memorial Field House. Groundbreaking was April 11, 2021, which would have been Maddie's twenty-first birthday. It was opened a year later on August 13, 2022.

More than three years after Maddie's death, Pat was honest in her reaction. "I cannot understand how an all-loving God can take such a child from those who loved her so much. He is not the God I grew up believing in. In time, I might be able to trust Him again. I might stop being so angry with Him, but I am not ready to do that."

Pat's reaction is not uncommon.

Writing in *Christianity Today* during the COVID-19 pandemic Baylor University Professor Perry L. Glanzer wrote about weathering a health crisis. "During my health problems, many of my prayers involved little more than yelling at God. If you have yelled at God, that's good. It means you are still living in relationship with Him, even amid extreme stress."

Among the yellers we read about in the Bible are King David and Jesus. At a low point in his life, David wrote in Psalm 22, "My God, my God, why have you forsaken me?" On the cross, Jesus repeated David's psalm. When we feel forsaken—and don't we all at times?—understand that David and Jesus went before us. Why has God allowed this to happen?

In the fall of 2020, Pat suffered another loss when her twin brother Butch, died at the age of seventy-three. Because he was hospitalized during the pandemic, Pat was not allowed to visit him or attend his private funeral. Unlike Maddie, he had had multiple health issues, including heart disease and diabetes, and for more than a year, Butch needed a walker.

Butch had lived a full life, and died in faith. Knowing how

he relied on the cross for his salvation, his family recognized his death as sweet relief. In the words of the Negro spiritual, he could, "Steal away to Jesus."

My sister Virginia Malwitz Gable was the youngest of the five Malwitz children. In her early fifties, she was diagnosed with ovarian cancer and suffered significantly. In October 2012, she was discharged from the hospital and moved to a bed in the sunroom of the home of my sister Dr. Alieta Malwitz Eck. Members of the family took turns sitting with her. Abby took a turn on October 14, a Sunday. I stayed with her that Monday.

About ten o'clock in the morning, Ginny said to me, barely above a whisper, "I can't take it anymore." Those would be her last words.

Around noon, Alieta came home to walk Ginny to the bathroom. Alieta called to say she needed help. Ginny died in the arms of her sister and brother. She was fifty-four and heaven bound.

CHAPTER 19

The Old Order Will Pass

A friend of mine who loves Jesus just as we do has a daughter with profound disabilities, far worse than anything Leah will go through. I asked him how his daughter's disability may have weakened or strengthened his faith. Yes, it is a challenge, he said, but it strengthened his focus on the hope of the believer. There will be a wonderful reckoning in heaven, he said.

He mentioned the promises at the end of the Bible. "[God] will wipe away every tear from their eyes. There will be no more death or mourning or crying or pain, for the old order of things has passed away" (Revelation 21:4).

In heaven, where there will be a new Jerusalem and a new earth, the Bible teaches us. "Those who are victorious will inherit all this, and I will be their God and they will be my children" (Revelation 21:7).

Who will "inherit all this"? Who goes to heaven?

The dominant belief in America today is that we achieve salvation by character. Good people go to heaven. There is someone like a cosmic Santa Claus keeping score, calculating who has been naughty or nice.

In 1927, prominent atheist Bertrand Russell gave a lecture in London that he titled *"Why I Am Not a Christian."* Of the label

"Christian" Russell said, "It is used these days in a very loose sense by a great many people. Some people mean no more by it than a person who attempts to live a good life."

Simple. Lead a good life, call yourself a good Christian (or a good Jew, or a good Muslim or an ethical Universalist), and you go to heaven when you die.

During our trip to Egypt in the spring of 2020, we learned how the ancient Egyptians believed your heart was lightened by charitable deeds. When you died, the god Osiris would put your heart on a balancing scale with an ostrich feather on the opposite side. If your heart was lighter than the feather, you sailed to a paradise known as the Field of Reeds. If your heart was heavier, you would be devoured by a crocodile named Ammit.

John Bunyan, author of *The Pilgrim's Progress*, recognized how his former faulty life was not leading him to paradise. He was Ammit bait. In his autobiography, *Grace Abounding to the Chief of Sinners,* Bunyan wrote, "But the sin and pollution I was born with—that was my great plague and affliction. I was more loathsome in my eyes than a toad, and I thought that I was the same way in God's eyes. I understood perfectly well that I needed to be presented without fault before God and this could only be done by Jesus Christ."

We all have faults, so who can stand? That is not simply hard; it is impossible. You need to be perfect, flawless, spotlessly clean to get into the heaven of the Bible. There is no scale weighing good versus evil and measuring it against an ostrich feather. In God's eyes, the wrong side of the natural man has the weight of the Colorado Rockies. The Bible says our righteousness—our good parts—are as "filthy rags."

English theologian Dr. David Martyn Lloyd-Jones, wrote in *The Cross: God's Way of Salvation*, "We deserve nothing but hell. If you think you deserve heaven, take it from me, you are not a Christian."

There is a tradition in Orthodox Judaism that requires a woman to take a mikvah, a bath with full immersion, prior to her wedding. Her skin must be flawless; she must wear no jewelry, no makeup.

In *Unorthodox,* the autobiography Deborah Feldman wrote after she left Orthodox Judaism, she explained how she prepared for her mikvah. She washed her hair twice, clipped her nails, made sure nothing was behind her ears, between her toes, or lodged in her belly button. She was told if there was something she may have missed, she had to begin the process all over again. "I don't want that, so I make sure I'm clean according to the law," Feldman wrote.

The Bible teaches that we must be perfectly clean to enter God's heaven. Orthodox Christianity teaches that only Jesus can make us clean. As nineteenth-century hymn writer Robert Lowry wrote, "What can wash away my sin? Nothing but the blood of Jesus." It is Jesus and only Jesus. "He who knew no sin became sin for us so that, in Him, we might become the righteousness of God" (2 Corinthians 5:21).

But what about all those good people who reject Jesus, who are relying on there being another way? The people with good character. In *Hugo Black of Alabama,* biographer Steve Suitts tells the story of Black, who served on the US Supreme Court from 1937 to 1971. The author identifies a man named Herman Beck who was a "father figure" to Hugo Black. Together, Hugo Black, Herman Beck, and a Methodist minister served in a fraternal organization.

Hugo Black reminded the minister that Herman Beck was a Jew who did not believe in Jesus as his personal savior. He wondered, *Does Herman Beck go to heaven?* The minister looked at Hugo Black and said he would not want to go to a heaven "that would not let Herman Beck in."

There is no reason to doubt Herman Beck was nothing but an honorable man. We all know Herman Becks who we would allow into our version of heaven, if only we were keeping score. But Jesus said in John 14:6, "I am the way, the truth and the life. No one comes to the Father *except through me*" (emphasis added).

You must be perfect to enter the heaven of the Bible, and to be perfect, you must be completely clean. There can be no lint in your belly button. According to Revelation 21:27, "Nothing impure will ever enter [heaven]."

The way I used to illustrate it was to talk about HIV, the virus that causes AIDS. You could have been a healthy, muscular ironworker, but if you were accidently pricked by a needle contaminated with HIV, invisible to the naked eye, the virus could poison your bloodstream and kill you. The COVID-19 virus gave us a more recent example.

The Bible teaches that sin entered the human race through Adam, who had been placed in the Garden of Eden. Adam and Eve were told by God the garden was all theirs, except for the tree of "the knowledge of good and evil, for when you eat from it you will certainly die" (Genesis 2:17).

The serpent told Eve that God prohibited them from eating the fruit of the tree because if they did, "you will be like God." Eve took the bite, gave the forbidden fruit to Adam, and he took a bite. When confronted, Adam blamed God and Eve. "The woman you put here with me—she gave me some fruit from the tree and I ate it" (Genesis 3:12).

If the Ligonier National Conference in Orlando in 2014 is remembered for one moment, it was when four Bible teachers answered random questions from conference-goers.

One questioner wondered if God was not being too severe when He punished humanity for a sin that seems so trivial. Taking a bite from the forbidden fruit seems about as heinous as a kid taking a cookie after mommy told him not to.

R.C. Sproul, one of the teachers, suggested that the anonymous questioner did not understand how sin, no matter how trivial, violates the holiness of God.

"And the punishment was too severe?" Sproul wondered.

"What's wrong with you people?" he thundered. (The quote has been memorialized on a coffee mug I have in our kitchen cabinet.)

Joe Hofmann was a colleague in the sports department at *The News Tribune* of Woodbridge in the 1980s. In the spring of 2021, he and his wife, Donna, received awful news from their son Joseph, who was returning from a trip to Maine with his brother Michael and two friends. Joseph called from an emergency room in New Hampshire. "He said, 'Dad we had an accident, and Mikey did not make it.'"

A woman's vehicle crossed a highway median and crashed into the Jeep that Joseph was driving. Doctors said twenty-seven-year-old Michael died on impact.

In an essay printed in the *Colonia Corner*, a local publication, Joe wrote, "We take great comfort in knowing that Mike is freed from his suffering and in eternal glory. The sin debt he owed God was paid at the cross by Jesus. There's nothing we can do to earn our salvation. It was the simple act of faith made possible only when Mike received Jesus into his heart. Mike's reward is that he now rests in eternal glory."

The Sunday before his son's death, Joe attended the Sunday service at Calvary Chapel in Old Bridge. At the end of a challenging sermon by lead pastor Lloyd Pulley, Joe prayed to God, "Use me. Use me. Use me."

He told me his essay was "My gospel message to Colonia. My prayer today is, 'Even so, come, Lord Jesus,' knowing I'll see Mikey again."

When the son born to Bathsheba died, King David, the child's father, "went into the house of the Lord and worshiped" (1 Samuel 12:20). His servants were puzzled. When the child was alive, he fasted and prayed. "Now that the child is dead, you get up and eat."

"He answered, 'While the child was still alive, I fasted and wept. I thought "Who knows?" The Lord may be gracious to me and let the child live. But now that he is dead why shall I fast? Can I bring him back again? I will go to him, but he will not return to me.'"

Michael J. Kruger wrote *Surviving Religion 101* in the form of an open letter to his daughter Emma before she enrolled in the University of North Carolina. He anticipated how some students will doubt the value of beliefs in God and Christianity because of suffering in the world. "Make no mistake about it, one of the biggest tests of any system of belief is whether it can provide real hope in the midst of a dark, broken world," he wrote.

"What is needed, therefore, is a solution to suffering that transcends this broken world. A solution that comes from *outside* the world. And this is the promise offered in the Christian worldview. There is also a deep and profound hope that someday God will set all these things right in eternity. Someday there will be a new world, in which the old order of things has passed away and a new order has come."

This is the hope that sustained my siblings when our sister Ginny died and sustained Joe Hofmann after his son's death.

In the summer of 2009 Rev. Bob Bashioum, the associate pastor at Grace Alliance Church in Piscataway, the church

Donna and I attend, sent an email to the congregation following a diagnosis of liver cancer: "I'm feeling fine, except for being very yellow and a little tired. But other than that, I have no complaints. God is revealing Himself to Shirl and me in remarkable ways and we're resting in Him. Even the ultrasound tech commented this evening how peaceful I was. Please pray that God would use my illness to bring people to salvation. I don't want to waste this illness." (He echoed Abby's prayer during the first week of Leah's illness: "This will not be wasted.")

When our pastor Rev. Mark Kincade emailed the congregation with news of Bob's death thirteen months after the diagnosis, he wrote, "Bob was an incredibly Godly man who served the Lord all his life, yet he did not think he deserved heaven. Instead, he was trusting in Jesus Christ, who had forgiven his sins and made him a child of God. He told me, 'I know beyond a shadow of doubt where I am going. I want everyone else to know about Jesus.'"

One month earlier he had told Mark that he was not afraid of dying, just the pain of it. "I can't wait to see what heaven looks like."

CHAPTER 20

Streets of Gold

What does Bob Bashioum now know that we don't know? What is behind those heavenly pearly gates?

Wallace and Minerva Wills were enslaved in the Choctaw Nation area of Oklahoma, working in cotton fields owned by a man named Britt Willis. According to the Oklahoma Historical Society, "Uncle Wallace composed 'plantation songs' as he worked in the fields. Aunt Minerva would sing along with him when they were asked to perform the songs for the students [at a local academy] in the evenings."

The couple was heaven-minded, composing some of the most well-known Negro spirituals: "Swing Low, Sweet Chariot"; "Roll, Jordan, Roll"; "I'm A-Rollin', I'm A-Rollin'"; "The Angels Are A-Comin'"; and "Steal Away to Jesus." The Jubilee Singers of Fisk University in Nashville sang these songs while touring the United States and Europe. It is said that during a performance in London, England's Queen Victoria requested an encore of "Steal Away to Jesus."

The popular image involves streets of gold, walls of jasper, and harps. What Wallace and Minerva Willis knew about heaven was that Jesus is there, and there are no scorching Oklahoma cotton fields to tend to.

In *"Roll, Jordan, Roll,"* former Rutgers University history professor Eugene Genovese wrote about Black slaves who worked in the big house, where the plantation owner lived. They resented having to stand whenever a white person entered the room. "The line in that spiritual that says 'I want to be in heaven sittin' down' particularly expresses the resentment of the house servants," Genovese wrote.

Heaven is sittin' down. In the book of Hebrews, the author used the word *rest* or *rested* nine times in the third and fourth chapters. "Now we who believe enter that rest" (Hebrews 4:3a).

So what is there there?

"Sometimes, especially in popular presentations, heaven is depicted primarily as a place of great physical pleasure, a place where everything we have desired here on earth is fulfilled to the ultimate degree. Thus, heaven seems to be merely earthly (even worldly) conditions amplified," wrote Millard J. Erickson in *Christian Theology*.

Some of my dreams of heaven have included playing baseball on an immaculate field with no bad bounces or playing a trumpet solo at Carnegie Hall in Handel's *Messiah*. Perhaps your dreams involve golf. The other day, Donna was insisting there will be fried green tomatoes in heaven.

Erickson continued, "The correct perspective, however, is to see the basic nature of heaven as the presence of God; from His presence all of the blessings of heaven follow. The presence of God means that we will have perfect knowledge."

In his book *The Redeemer's Return*, Arthur W. Pink (1886-1952) quoted an author he identified as W. Trotter: "Man was not made for the present, and the present was not made to satisfy man. It is for the future, not the present, that man exists."

When our son was deciding among colleges to attend, we visited the University of Pennsylvania in Philadelphia. Our student escort pointed to a drab-looking dormitory and told us that was where Donald Trump Jr. lived. And here I'm thinking, *Not for long.* Someone soon that young man will have his choice of a waterfront mansion or a deluxe apartment in the sky. The dorm was not his home.

During his final week on earth, Jesus said, "My Father's house has many rooms, if that were not so, would I have told you that I am going there to prepare a place for you?" (John 14:2).

For believers, the hope of heaven is often most real in the worst of times.

Bob Grahmann, who grew up in Woodbridge, has been a friend for more than fifty years. He is a longtime staff member of Intervarsity Christian Fellowship, an organization that serves university students. He served as director of the International Fellowship of Evangelical Students and lived in Kyiv, Ukraine, in the early 2000s.

Soon after the Russian invasion of Ukraine, he told the story of an IFES staff woman named Anna who was five months pregnant and living with her husband in a small village in the Carpathian Mountains. Bob asked his supporters to pray for her health and the safe delivery of the baby.

"I wrote to Anna on Sunday to wish her a happy Easter, and she wrote back today and said this: 'Easter this year has a special meaning of hope. Because it's one more reminder that even if Putin makes it impossible for me to come back to my home in Kyiv and to my parents' home in Kharkiv, he has no power to take away my home in heaven! That's what I have been thinking these last weeks before Easter.'"

Anna was a living testimony to words of the apostle Paul, who wrote to Christians who experienced severe persecution in the first century, "I consider that our present sufferings are not worth comparing with the glory that will be revealed in us" (Romans 8:18).

Hopefully Leah will exceed my three score and fourteen years and live a long and fruitful life on earth. She and her siblings and her cousins have a good chance to live into the twenty-second century. But even then, their lives will be a blip compared with eternity. As Erwin W. Lutzer noted, "There is no such thing as half an eternity."

I smile when someone posts an entry on social media about how Uncle Fred, who died a year ago, is celebrating "his first birthday in heaven." No, it's we who are celebrating, and only here on earth. There are no August 25ths in heaven. Nor was there a Y2K. We can picture streets of gold, but we cannot comprehend heaven without time. "When we've been there ten thousand years," as John Newton wrote in the hymn "Amazing Grace," we will not pause to mark the occasion. What are ten thousand years when there is no sun to revolve around every 365 days?

Speaking of heaven, Puritan author Stephen Charnock (1628–1680) wrote in *The Existence and Attributes of God*, "Death is a word never spoken there by any; never heard by any in that possession of eternity; it is forever put out as one of God's conquered enemies. The happiness depends on the presence of God, with whom believers shall be ever present. Happiness cannot perish as long as God lives."

Charnock added, "God is always vigorous and flourishing, a pure act of life sparking new fresh rays of life and light to the creature, flourishing with perpetual spring, and contenting the most capricious desire, forming your interest, pleasure and satisfaction, with infinite variety. He will have variety to increase delights and eternity to perpetuate them."

Once, I flew out of Newark Liberty International Airport

on a gloomy day. About ten minutes into the flight, the airplane rose above the clouds into bright sunlight. A little girl of about six in the row behind me asked her mother, "Is this heaven?"

Heaven forbid, I thought. My vision of The Other Place is spending eternity in seat 27D, living on little pretzels and Diet Coke, an endless loop of one dreadful movie on the small screen, with no reading material except an in-flight magazine. ("For me," wrote N.T. Wright, "hell is the incomprehensible instructions that come with flat-back furniture.")

In *Surprised by Suffering*, R.C. Sproul wrote, "One sage remarked that if we were to imagine the most pleasant experience possible and thought about doing that for eternity, we would be conceiving of something that would be closer to hell than to heaven."

Like a thug named Rocky.

In an episode of *The Twilight Zone* that aired on April 15,1960, a character named Rocky Valentine robbed a pawnshop and killed a man before being shot to death. When he came to, he was met by Pip, who Rocky believed to be his guardian angel. Pip escorted him to a deluxe apartment, bringing him to a pool hall where Rocky was surrounded by gorgeous women, and when he played billiards, he never lost. He assumed he was in heaven.

Rocky was soon tired of all the winning. When all his wishes came true, he was bored. There were no losses, no agony of defeat. "I don't belong in heaven, see? I want to go to The Other Place," he told Pip.

"Heaven? Whatever gave you the idea that you were in heaven, Mr. Valentine? This *is* The Other Place!"

Then narrator Rod Serling explained: "A scared, angry little man who never got a break. Now he has everything he's ever wanted, and he's going to have to live with it for eternity—in The Twilight Zone."

Actually, the biblical understanding of The Other Place is gnashing of teeth and a lake of fire. There are no pool halls. They don't serve breakfast in hell.

CHAPTER 21

Small-Town America

The image I started with—four guys holding four corners of a discarded sail, lowering a paralytic to Jesus through a hole in the roof—began with the family and church each holding a corner. Grabbing the third corner was the community of Long Hill Township.

Long Hill Township, with a population of about 8,500, is the type of town where kids know kids and parents know parents through the rec leagues, the Girl Scouts, the schools, the coffee line at Panera, and the grocery aisles at the ShopRite.

If what you know about New Jersey is the view from the New Jersey Turnpike or Northeast Corridor railroads, or dialogue from *The Sopranos* or *Jersey Shore*, fuhgeddaboudit.

Long Hill, as the name gives hint, is part of the Watchung Mountains. It includes a sizable portion of the Great Swamp National Wildlife Refuge, with the historic Passaic River running adjacent to the local baseball and softball complex, occasionally flooding the fields in the spring. During the Ice Age, the Wisconsin Glacier extended from Duluth, Minnesota, to Long Island, famously forming the Great Lakes. The ice receded about forty thousand years ago, leaving behind in New Jersey what geologists call Lake Passaic, a remnant of which evolved into what is now the fifty-five-square-mile Great Swamp that drains into the Passaic River, which meanders north to the Great Falls in Paterson to industrial Newark and out to sea.

The township was known as Passaic Township until 1992, when residents voted by a narrow margin to change the name to Long Hill Township, eliminating confusion with the city of Passaic, twenty-two miles to the north. According to former Police Chief Ahmed Naga, the department would occasionally get emergency calls about incidents on Passaic Avenue and had to tell the caller that the Passaic Avenue liquor store was in the *city* of Passaic.

The Gladstone Branch of the NJ Transit rail system has three Long Hill stops, in Millington, Stirling, and Gillette, giving the small town three zip codes. The Hansens live in Gillette. George Howell was an engineer who surveyed the area for the former New Jersey West Line Railroad, and he named a train station after his fiancée, Rachel Gillette. (In lieu of flowers perhaps?) When the company that makes Gillette razors considered moving its headquarters to its namesake community, the idea met resistance from residents, who did not envision their section of town becoming a major corporate home.

When Abby and Peter were married, they lived first in an apartment in Madison and almost immediately began looking for a home of their own, somewhere between Peter's job in Randolph, Abby's job teaching in Green Brook, and their extended families. The house they would find is 13.4 Google Maps miles from Art and Ann Hansen, and 12.9 Google Maps miles from Donna and I.

Abby was vaguely familiar with Long Hill because it is one of four towns that sends students from the ninth to twelfth grades to Watchung Hills Regional High School. The other three sending towns are Green Brook, where she taught, Warren, and Watchung.

They settled on a Cape Cod house in the Gillette section, with first-floor living space, an unfinished second floor, and a backyard jungle of cedar trees. In short order, they removed most of the trees, renovated the kitchen, added three bedrooms to the second floor, and finished the basement. When they converted the house from oil heat to gas, Peter was skilled enough to do the work himself.

From the time Leah was able to walk, Abby began signing her up for *everything*: softball, soccer, field hockey, basketball. It was a pattern she would repeat with Timmy, Joey, and Serena. The kids participated in about all the township has to offer, including the Easter egg hunt, the Halloween parade, and the traditional Memorial Day parade. Leah thrived in softball, playing in the local rec league and for the Long Hill Twisters travel team.

Abby and Leah made two of their most enduring friendships when Abby took Leah, then a preschooler, to the public library, where they met Emily Caputo and her daughter Maggie. "They were babies when we took them to programs at the library. That's how we met," said Emily. "Abby and I found out we had a lot in common, starting with the babies and the library. God put us in each other's lives."

In 2011, when her daughter was two years old, Emily suffered a stroke during surgery. When Leah suffered her spinal cord stroke in 2018, Maggie had a rare understanding. Emily and her daughter had a vocabulary. "Maggie remembered when I couldn't walk, couldn't feed myself, was going to rehab and was not looking like her mother."

Emily would make what my wife, Donna, calls "a remarkable

recovery. She did great in rehab." Donna mentioned this when Leah was doing great in rehab.

Emily drew on her own recovery story when Leah suffered a spinal cord stroke. "Maggie and I had this hope right away. God can work miracles. I'm taken aback when I see her. She's so strong, so courageous. She has so much hope."

Leah and Maggie would be in Mrs. Jenifer Clark's kindergarten class at Gillette School, and together Abby and Emily started a Girl Scout Daisy troop for their kindergarten girls.

In the summer of 2021, Leah went to Tapawingo, a Christian camp for girls between nine and seventeen, affiliated with Camp of the Words, in Speculator, New York. With Art and Ann Hansen owning a home nearby, Leah had known from infancy there was a girls' camp on an island in Lake Pleasant. By the time she was twelve, Abby thought Leah could meet the test of being a camper. The following summer, Abby sold Emily on having Maggie join Leah at camp. "I signed her up without even asking her," said Emily.

CHAPTER 22

'The Happiest Kid'

L eah spent three years in the Little Footprints preschool program at Millington Baptist Church. Fixed on my retirement schedule was a weekly date with her, picking her up at the church basement and doing lunch together at Burger King, where we had our special table.

Then, in September 2014, she was ready for the big leagues, when she would attend kindergarten at Gillette School. On the first day of school, Abby posted on social media a picture of Leah, with her pink backpack, getting on the bus to take her to kindergarten. Abby explained she had four kids. But on this day, she wrote, "My whole heart belongs to Leah."

"She was the happiest kid. She thrived in the school setting," said Jenifer Clark, her kindergarten teacher. "She was passionate about it all. Kids come in reserved or ready to go. Leah was definitely ready to go."

Two years later, Mrs. Clark would be Timmy's kindergarten teacher. In the fall of 2018, she would teach Serena and Joey. Twins are typically separated when there is more than one kindergarten class, but with Abby's blessing, both were assigned to Mrs. Clark. After the trauma of Leah's illness, she and Abby thought it best to have the twins with a familiar teacher who had become a close family friend. "I knew what they were going through. They had a background with me. With everything going on, it was helpful for the whole family," said Mrs. Clark. "We [including her husband, Joe] got really close to Leah's parents. We were able to form a nice friendship with them."

Mrs. Clark was teaching in the same building where she attended school. "My kindergarten class is where my daughter Elizabeth is now," she said in 2019. I can't tell you how many kids I've had in my classroom whose parents I knew from when we were kids. People do leave Long Hill. But when they have children, they seem to come back."

After kindergarten and first grade at Gillette School, Leah went to Millington School, where she would spend her next four years. "She was a firecracker from day one," said Jen Tremarco, her second-grade teacher.

Teachers are not supposed to play favorites, but they are like the rest of us; they do have favorites, and teachers came to lean on Leah. "She was a helper in the classroom. She was always the one assisting others. Now, seeing people helping her is flipping the role," said Miss Tremarco, who explained having Leah in her classroom was almost like having an extra aide. "If I had a hiccup, Leah would say, 'Miss T, we're doing this now.'"

"She was always helping others get their work done, and I'd have to say, 'OK now, Leah, it's time to get your work done,'" said Noelle Milito, who was Leah's third-grade teacher during the year she suffered the spinal cord stroke. Mrs. Milito said she considers it part of her job to act motherly to her students. "Leah was a second mom, my right-hand woman."

The first Sunday in March 2018, Mrs. Clark helped run a softball clinic that Leah attended and Leah was an eager participant. That Tuesday morning Mrs. Clark was in her kindergarten class when she received a text message from Abby about Leah being in the Morristown Medical Center, unable to breathe or move on her own. "You thought, *What in the world? Sunday she's hitting the ball, pitching the ball, and now she can't move?* I know it turned your family upside down," Mrs. Clark told me. "It turned a lot of people upside down."

Mrs. Milito thought hard that week, wondering if she missed a sign that something was wrong with Leah. Karen Freeman, the nurse, had not seen Leah in her office that day. Ten days later, when she learned Leah had suffered a spinal cord stroke, she was as puzzled as all of us. "I had not known anything about that condition. Ever. It was a sudden shock."

After getting the news, Mrs. Clark contacted Jaime Falvey, with whom she coached Leah's softball team, and they asked each other what could be done. "We knew immediately there was this family that needed help. There were other kids at home; a meal train had to be started." Coach Jaime began a GoFundMe campaign to raise money for anticipated out-of-pocket expenses that would be significant. The fund would exceed $28,000.

Early that first week, Mrs. Clark and Coach Jaime and their husbands went to the hospital, thinking they might not be allowed in the room. Abby welcomed them, and there was Leah, sedated, unable to talk, and hooked up to various machines. Mrs. Clark remembers hearing how doctors were puzzled. "They couldn't believe how bad she was. They were talking about how this was something they had never seen before."

On an early visit, Mrs. Clark kissed Leah on the forehead, leaving a lipstick mark. "The next time I came in, I said, 'Leah, should I kiss you again?' She blinked. That meant yes." On another visit, Mrs. Clark recalled, Leah struggled to pick up a Goldfish snack with her right hand. "She pushed herself. She was always a driven kid."

Miss Tremarco remembered those visits to Leah's room at the hospital. "You want to cry because that's not the Leah you had in the classroom. You saw that helpless body, and she was the complete opposite of that."

Mrs. Milito's class made get-well cards and birthday cards for Leah, who would be turning nine on March 15. "She was sick, and we're going to think of her in the most positive way possible." The class made a video in the school's library and sent it to Abby, but Abby did not show it to Leah, reasoning it would be too emotional for her.

Teachers and staff at Millington School regularly received emails from Jennifer Dawson, the principal, and Ed Acevedo, the superintendent of schools. They explained that one of Millington School's students was in the PICU in Morristown but could not be too specific—in part because of confidentiality rules and, in truth, because there was no diagnosis. "They couldn't explain too much because no one knew. They told us to keep Leah in our thoughts and prayers," said Mrs. Milito.

Leah's teachers were kept in the loop by Mrs. Clark, who typically opened a text message from Abby first thing in the morning. She found herself fearing the latest news during the harrowing first few days and then being encouraged as Leah improved.

Mrs. Dawson recalled how Leah's illness brought out the best in the staff and the community. "Jeni Clark was our go-between with Abby. The moms from school, from her softball team, were on top of everything."

Mrs. Milito told the third-grade students to come to her if they had questions. "Some of the girls had trouble coping with what was happening with their friend. There was just so much uncertainty. Usually, I have an answer for everything. It's part of my job. It was frustrating not knowing."

Mrs. Milito kept Leah's desk as it was, hoping she would be able to return sometime in the school year. Leah would return in June, hardly missing a beat. Abby and tutors at Children's Specialized Hospital had kept her up to speed.

That school year, she was one of about 380 students at Millington School but not well known by Mrs. Dawson, the principal. "Sometimes I get very familiar with students because they visit me, because they were sent to me. Leah was not one of them."

Over the summer, Mrs. Dawson assigned Leah to Beth Franco's fourth-grade class. (In the following spring, she became Beth Fischer, at a wedding Leah and other girls in the class attended with their mothers). "I remember telling Miss Franco that Leah was good about speaking for herself," said Mrs. Dawson. "She was our superstar student. I told Leah if something was too difficult, ask your teacher for help. 'No, I'm good,' Leah told me."

Mrs. Dawson recalled how she told her personal physician in Somerville about a student at school who had an illness that no one ever heard about. "Every time I see that doctor, she asks, 'How's that little girl doing?' There was concern that she may never walk again, and here she is."

September 2018, at the start of the new school year, Mrs. Dawson was amazed by how well Leah looked. "When she came bounding up the stairs, I was just blown away. *Wow, this is so different.* It was like night and day. She was more stable. I didn't worry about her falling. I remember Abby saying, 'If she falls, she will get back up.'"

Mrs. Fischer said Leah needed a little extra time to get settled in the morning and occasionally had to stand because she became stiff after sitting too long. "She sits next to her friend Matthew, and he's awesome. When I say we need to take out a special notebook, he automatically helps her. She takes the help because it moves things along," said Mrs. Franco.

The alphabet put Leah Hansen and Matthew Hubert side by side when the school year began, and he became her helper without being asked. Every marking period, Mrs. Fischer rearranged the desks, but after briefly separating Leah and Matthew, she realized her mistake and returned them to adjacent desks. "Matthew has been amazing. She doesn't think anything of it. He doesn't think anything of it. It's just what they do."

"Matthew likes to treat people kindly, and he expects the same from others," said his father, Joe Hubert.

It was not just Matthew, said Mrs. Fischer. "Other kids help Leah whenever they can. There's no obstacle she cannot do. She's making it work. She's proud that this happened to her, and she has overcome it. Everybody knows what happened, but it is not affecting her. She's such a sweet girl, very meticulous. She takes pride in her work. She wants to make it perfect."

"I do believe in the innate goodness in people, in children," said Mrs. Freeman, the nurse. "They designate themselves Leah's helper."

"Leah did not hide her illness," said Mrs. Fischer. One day students were discussing the blizzard the previous March that closed school for a week. "Leah said, 'I don't remember that. I was in the hospital.'"

According to Mrs. Fischer, the boy who mentioned the blizzard said, "'Oh, I'm sorry, I didn't realize that.' He was apologizing for bringing it up. Leah said it was OK. She's so sweet and positive. Your daughter [Abby] too. They're so positive about everything, not just this."

CHAPTER 23

Strong Like a Girl

Tim Simo has known the Hansen family since his daughter Sienna and Leah attended the Little Footprints preschool and the two played softball together. Simo's son Brady plays youth league baseball with Timmy. "School and sports have been a great way of connection," said Simo, a high school softball, basketball, and football coach.

On the day Leah got sick, Simo was at the playground watching the two girls play. The next day, he received sketchy news that something had happened to Leah, that she felt numbness and had trouble walking. He was certain nothing had occurred on the playground. "Then we started getting bits and pieces from people in the community that it was much more serious [than numbness]."

Once the seriousness was known, like many in the Long Hill community, he decided he wanted to do whatever he could to help the Hansen family.

The softball team he coached at Summit High School had a scrimmage scheduled with the team from Watchung Hills Regional High. "I called their athletic director to see if we could turn [the scrimmage] into a fundraiser. He was OK." Simo thought the fundraiser could draw attention to whatever

146

disease had caused Leah's illness, though, like the rest of us, he didn't know what the disease was.

The weather in Central New Jersey in the spring of 2018 was a problem, with steady rains and occasional wet snow turning dirt fields into mud. Conditions at the Watchung Hills home field would be a problem.

Watchung Hills Coach Brett Picaro contacted MaryAnne DeFinis, the president of the Watchung Hills Softball Booster Club, knowing she had friends on the staff at Diamond Nation in Flemington, a baseball and softball complex with an abundance of fields that have artificial turf.

DeFinis, whose daughter Isabella played on the 2016 Watchung Hills state championship softball team, was aware of the story of a local girl who had suffered a spinal cord stroke but was short on details. She was motivated to act the moment Simo sent her a portrait of Leah. "When I saw the picture of her, my heart sank. How could you not fall in love with that girl?" said DeFinis.

Diamond Nation is a partnership between Jack Cust and Jennie Finch. Cust, a graduate of Immaculata High School in Somerville, played parts of ten seasons in Major League Baseball. Finch pitched for the USA team that won an Olympic gold medal in 2004. She had sent Leah an autographed jersey and an autographed softball inscribed: "To Leah, Wishing you all the best! Much love & prayers. You can do it, Phil 4:13." The Bible verse from Philippians reads: "I can do everything through Him who gives me strength." (When Leah was hospitalized in New Brunswick, Finch was a competitor on *Dancing with the Stars*, giving the hospital floor a rooting interest.)

Nick Massari, the general manager at Diamond Nation, said the complex embraced the idea. "Leah Hansen is part of the softball community, and that makes her a teammate of all of us who love the sport," he told the *Courier News* of Somerville.

The booster club purchased jerseys for the players from Summit and Watchung Hills. Each had "Hansen No. 1" on the back. The club also obtained red T-shirts for kids attending the game with the message "Strong Like A Girl" on the front and "Hansen No. 1" on the back.

The T-shirts were created by Jon Seccamanie, who works with a sporting goods company. He and his wife Dawn knew the Hansens from the time their daughter Jayden played softball with Leah, and they had visited Leah at the Morristown hospital.

Buses were leased to take more than thirty students to the game. Jaime Falvey helped to arrange for them to leave school early for the thirty-mile trip to Diamond Nation.

It was a damp day, when playing on the grass field at Watchung Hills would have been impossible. The day had a carnival atmosphere. Forty-two kids posed for a group photo on an adjacent field, posing in their "Strong Like A Girl" tees.

The "Strong Like A Girl" motto had been adopted by Leah. The Friday before Leah got sick, her aunt Carrie had gone to Mrs. Milito's third-grade class to read a book as part of the Dr. Seuss reading program. Kids were encouraged to wear shirts with writing on the front. While Leah was hospitalized in Morristown, Carrie and Abby were trying to remember what was on her shirt. They were stumped, until Leah mouthed the words "Strong. Like. A. Girl." The motto stuck and was shortened to SLAG.

With the high school girls in their Hansen uniforms and dozens of kids in their SLAG T-shirts, Peter was joined at the pitcher's mound by Timmy, Joey, and Serena. Timmy threw out the ceremonial first pitch, throwing a strike to Summit catcher Taylor Thompson, who later told Coach Simo, "That was one of the most nerve-racking yet most rewarding experiences I ever had—catching the first pitch from a family going through what they're going through."

Watchung Hills Coach Picaro said his team was anxious—first of all to play on the artificial turf during the soggy spring before an enthusiastic crowd, and then to help the Hansen family. "It was something different, something special," he said.

Joe Shaw, who scheduled umpires for games involving the Skyland Conference—my assignor for ten years when I umpired high school baseball—assigned himself to umpire behind the plate. "What I remember about that day was being impressed by the young people on both teams doing all they could, supporting your granddaughter. The coaches were congratulated by me and [fellow umpire] Bob Varju on teaching the girls how important it is to give back."

Coach Simo arranged for "Hansen No. 1" decals to be given to all players on the twenty-six high school varsity softball teams in Union County.

The softball family would be broadened to include the team at Rutgers, after its softball coach, Jay Nelson, reached out to Coach Simo, offering his assistance. Members of the Rutgers softball team visited Leah at Children's Specialized Hospital in New Brunswick, bringing with them a poster autographed by the players.

When Coach Simo and his wife, Ashley, visited Leah, it was difficult to reconcile the fact that the girl motionless in the hospital bed was the same girl who'd been doing cartwheels days before the onset of numbness. "I remember Abby telling me, 'She's going to walk again. She's going to run again. She's going to throw a softball again.' Not everybody can have that strength. Pete and Abby have been so positive for Leah's sake."

*"Strong Like a Girl" Long Hill Community rallying
to encourage Leah, Spring, 2018*

CHAPTER 24

Weekend to Remember

The January 31, 2019, issue of the *Echoes-Sentinel*, a weekly newspaper that covers Long Hill Township, was one for the family scrapbook.

Page 1 had a good news story below the fold about Leah and the local talent show, and a better news story above the fold that involved the five-year-old Hansen twins.

The good news headline: "Talent show a rousing success." It told the story of the Long Hill's Got Talent program held at the Watchung Hills Regional High School auditorium.

"The most moving act of the night was a number, set to Rachel Platten's hit song *Fight Song*, performed by 38 fourth- and fifth-grade girls from Millington School—teammates from the Long Hill Twisters softball team and fellow Girl Scouts who celebrated the perseverance of classmates Leah Hansen and Grace Eline," wrote *Echoes-Sentinel* reporter Claudia Ceva.

The stories of Leah and Grace were well known by classmates, their parents, and the Long Hill community. Leah was recovering from a spinal cord stroke diagnosed the previous March. Grace was recovering from a tumor on her brain, diagnosed one month later.

"I wanted to take their stories and try to make them come to life on stage," said Darcy Carn, a professional dance instructor who worked with Abby to create choreography for the event.

The performance ended with the fathers of Leah and Grace, in formal wear, lifting their daughters, in formal dress, as half the girls behind them wore red "Strong Like A Girl" T-shirts in support of Leah, and the other half wore green "Good Vibe Warrior" T-shirts in support of Grace. The girls shadow-boxed with boxing gloves to the tune of "Fight Song."

> This is my fight song, Take back my life song. Prove I'm alright song. My power's turned on. Starting right now I'll be strong. I'll play my fight song, And I don't care if nobody else believes. 'Cause I've still got a lot of life in me.

Carn recalled how Leah and Grace played important roles in the numerous practices. "Leah, as fit her personality, took a leadership role. Those two girls never sat down, even when they were not needed in the production. They have a very tight friendship. It helps to have your best friend with you."

"There is no tangible way to repay the many angels, but I wanted to try," Abby told the *Echoes-Sentinel*. "When Leah and Grace walked out on that stage, I wanted the many cheerleaders to sit back and recognize the huge role they played."

During the background music of "Fight Song," images of Leah and Grace were shown on the big screen above them. The routine ended with the girls, wearing boxing gloves, spelling out, in big letters: LONGHILLSTRONG.

Absent that night was Grace's mother, Aubrey, who was in Switzerland at a business conference she had committed to attend. She would not see the performance until Abby sent her a link the next morning. There was something else on her plate that night.

"At 10:30 [Switzerland time], I got a call from a speechwriter at the White House," Aubrey recalled. Grace was invited to Washington by the office of President Donald J. Trump, who would mention her in the State of the Union address while she sat next to Melania Trump. The president explained how Grace joined an effort to fight against cancer, raising $40,000 for the Valerie Fund, a charity that supports children with cancer.

"I was thinking, *Wow, it's the president, and he's actually talking about me*," Grace told the *Daily Record* of Morristown, speaking on a cell phone on the drive home from Washington.

In the spring, Grace and Leah and their moms got invitations to a Taylor Swift concert at MetLife Stadium in East Rutherford, New Jersey, and together they have participated in fundraising events.

The talent show was the feel-good story below the fold of the *Echoes-Sentinel*. Above the fold was an even better story: "Students unharmed in bus crash."

There was nothing good about the crash, except the safe landing. The story was accompanied by a picture of a yellow school bus that had careened into a ditch, with a utility pole and wires dangling over the top of it.

Of the eight students on the bus, two were the Hansen twins, Serena and Joey. In an image from news helicopters, taken before the children were allowed to leave the bus, Serena's pink backpack was visible in the window. In a later image, Joey was seen walking to an ambulance, wearing his familiar red winter coat, carrying a paper bag with items that would be used for a Valentine's Day project.

The story received significant coverage on local television news, with a fifteen-second version on *ABC World News Tonight with David Muir*, accompanied by the image of the yellow school bus in a ditch.

Bus 11 routinely picked up the Hansens' next-door neighbors and then picked up the twins. Leah would have been on that bus, except ten months after the stroke, Abby was still driving her to Millington School. Every day, Timmy had a choice of the bus or mom's van. This day, he chose mom's van, a choice he would later regret.

As Abby prepared to drive to Millington School, she got a text alert from Channel 4, the local NBC affiliate. There was a school bus accident somewhere in New Jersey. "Of course, I ignored it," Abby said. New Jersey has countless yellow school buses on the road on a typical morning. What were the odds?

Then, during her drive, the sky above Long Hill was thumping with state police and news helicopters. The streets were busy with sirens from police and emergency vehicles. Abby then got a text from the school system about an accident involving bus 11. She did not know the twins' bus had a number.

Bob English, captain of the Long Hill First Aid Squad, was the initial first responder on the scene, after hearing about the accident on the police scanner. He rushed to the hilly intersection of Martinsville and Long Hill Roads. *This could be bad*, he thought, with wires strewn across the bus. English, a former professor of engineering at New Jersey Institute of Technology, recognized danger. When emergency crews arrive they must assume the wires are live and dangerous.

English ducked under the wires and looked into the open door. "I was yelling at the kids. 'Stay on the bus!'" The driver and students did not look as if they had been injured, but they would have not recognized the risk of downed wires. "Kids don't know the danger," he said.

But, said Police Chief Ahmed Naga, "Kids especially understand people in uniform are there to help. Those kids listening to instructions did not put first responders in jeopardy.

They listened very well. You could see the fear on them, at the same time you're telling them it's OK."

An employee of Jersey Central Power & Light Co. happened upon the scene as part of his morning commute and gave a quick assessment. He said it was still too risky to get the kids from the bus. At 8:54 a.m., a crew from JCP&L arrived, and by 8:57 a.m., they were able to give an all-clear. English told the kids it was safe to leave the bus. "They were giving me high fives," he said.

The bus driver, a sixty-three-year-old woman from Irvington, was given two summonses, for an improper left turn and for careless driving. She gave police permission to inspect her cell phone, and it indicated she was not using it at the time of the accident. A background check showed she had not been in an accident since 2004, and her only moving violation happened in 1994. (My driving record should be so good.)

Jeff Wanamaker, a career firefighter in Millburn and volunteer firefighter in Long Hill, participated in the rescue. When Joey left the bus, he said, "Hi, Mister Jeff." Joey knew Wanamaker, who was an assistant coach on Leah's softball team. Serena met him when he gave the Daisies, the littlest Girl Scouts, a tour of the fire station. He also had spoken to the twins' kindergarten class on safety. Wanamaker arranged for the kids to get a citation for courage at a Township Council meeting. Years later, Joey would say, "Courageous? I was terrified."

Lisa Scanlon, the township recreation director and a member of the EMT squad, heard about the accident on her police scanner. She hustled home to put on her uniform and then drove an ambulance to the scene. She was assigned to take the twins to Gillette School. "Both Serena and Joey were very brave and listened very well to all the instructions when they got off the bus. I asked them if they had ever been in an ambulance, and they said no. When they got in, they automatically put on their seat belts."

She asked the twins if she should sound the siren. Of course, they said yes. "They were absolutely in awe of the flashing lights. They were totally adorable," said Scanlon.

Abby learned that bus 11 was the twins' bus, once the danger had passed, when she received a text message from Mrs. Clark, their kindergarten teacher. She told Abby the kids were safe and the nurse had given them a clean bill of health.

Mrs. Clark sent Abby a text message with a photo of the twins, smiling with thumbs up. She then called Abby and put the twins on the phone. "They were both relieved to hear Mom's voice. I invited Abby to come down to give them a hug."

Abby went but not without an incident. As she rushed to the school, holding her cell phone while driving, she was stopped by a police officer. "My kids were on that bus!" she yelled. The officer excused the offense and let her go.

The one regret of the day was Timmy's. "I wish I could turn back time and be on the bus," he said that afternoon. Had Timny been there, he would have certainly offered a dramatic moment-by-moment version of events to News 4 New York. The next day, for the first time all school year, Leah took bus 11, joining Tim, Serena, and Joey. The replacement bus had a new driver, and police escorted the bus with flashing lights.

Two stories in the local weekly: the talent show and bus 11. Together they are what makes up a community: the schools, the softball teams, the talent show, the municipal workers, the volunteers, and a small-town weekly newspaper to tell the stories. "It was a community doing what communities do," said police Chief Naga.

CHAPTER 25

Twisters

On April 9, 2019, thirteen months after Leah suffered the spinal cord stroke, she would return to her field of dreams—the softball and baseball fields at the end of Poplar Drive in Long Hill, the home away from home for the Hansen kids.

That spring, Leah would play with the Comets; Timmy, the Braves; Joey, the Angels; and Serena, the Emeralds. The teams were formed in March, and Brian Sekeres, head coach of the Comets, was glad to draft Leah Hansen. Peter told Coach Brian that it would OK if Leah did not go on the field to play defense. Oh, no, said the coach. Leah would be a complete player, batting and playing defense, using a glove Peter modified with duct tape and Velcro.

Though Leah was in the fourth grade, an allowance was made for her to play with second and third graders. "She called herself, 'The Elder,'" said Coach Brian.

In her first game, on her second at bat, she hit a weak ground ball. A player on the other team failed to make the play, and Leah reached first base safely. On subsequent plays, she advanced to second, third, and home, scoring a run in a Comets' one-run victory.

When the Comets took the field, after Leah had rounded the bases, she was alone in the dugout, struggling to get the glove on her left hand. Assistant Coach Jeff Wanamaker offered to help. "No, I'm good," said Leah.

Coach Jeff, whose daughter Kathryn had been Leah's teammate on three different teams, saw something special in Leah. "I've been a career firefighter for thirty years, and I have never seen anyone braver than Leah Hansen. I'm not her dad, but I could not be prouder to see what she is accomplishing."

The fields at the end of Poplar Drive are the Hansens' playground. On Mother's Day in 2019, Peter said at least one of the kids either had a game or a practice on sixteen of the next seventeen days. After being idle in the spring of 2020 due to the pandemic, the three younger Hansens were active again in 2021, while Leah worked in the snack shop.

The Poplar Drive complex is on land donated by the township in the 1970s. Scott Lavender, former president of the association, explained, "Parents do all the work. We are a central part of the culture of Long Hill. This is small-town America at its best. People get to know each other down there at the fields."

One of the most difficult days for Abby and Leah had been the day the season opened in April 2018, one month after the stroke, when they were holed up in the hospital. Timmy, Joey, and Serena marched in uniform to the fields with their team. When the teams and coaches were introduced at the field, Leah's absence was noted, and at the mention of her name, there was sustained applause. Then a cheer was begun by girls in right field. "LE-AH HAN-SEN, LE-AH HAN-SEN." Once again, Timmy threw out a ceremonial first pitch.

Beginning at the age of seven, Leah was a member of the Twisters, a softball travel team. Coach Jaime Falvey recalled sending instructional videos to girls interested in softball, and Peter and Leah absorbed as much as they could. When the fall season began, Peter was one of the dads preparing the field as early as 6:00 a.m. on game days. "He was a major guy, every Saturday morning, all fall," said Coach Jaime.

Leah pitched for the Twisters, and her friend Maddie Falvey played first base. "There was no getting by that combination. Leah and Maddie were a magnetic duo," said Coach Jaime, an all-state second baseman for Watching Hills Regional High School in the mid-1990s. "Leah reminded me of me."

Coach Jaime visited Leah several times in the Morristown hospital. On one early visit, she remembered, "They placed a ball in her hand and said, 'Show them how Coach Jaime told you how to grip a ball.' No one knew what was happening, and it was not good. But cognitively, she was with it."

Coach Jaime was not surprised by the community support of Leah and her family. "Let's be honest, you create that for yourself. We have said multiple times, 'If this happened to any of us, Pete and Abby would do the same thing.' Even though I'm so sad this had to happen to Leah, so many positive things have come out of it. I think that's how we get through this. We think about the obstacles, at such a young age, but there is nothing that is going to stop this girl in her life. That's her. That's Leah."

The family, the church, and the community account for three of the guys holding corners of that old sail, borrowing an image from the story of four men cutting a hole in the roof of a crowded house in Capernaum, to lower a paralytic man to Jesus, who would heal him.

Leah is part of an exceptional family, and she had support from an engaged church and vibrant community. However, there would not be a book with the title *Little Girl, Get Up* without the medical community. Without that community, she would not have survived the first twelve hours.

Theirs is a story that brings us back to the beginning, to Genesis, the first chapter of the Bible.

CHAPTER 26

His Creatures

On the sixth day of creation, according to the biblical account in Genesis, after creating the sun, the stars, vegetation, and living creatures that crawl, the Godhead said, "Let us make mankind in our image and likeness."

God gave mankind dominion over the earth with the ability to do what no other creature could: accumulate knowledge and pass it on to the next generation. From day one, the beaver knew how to build a dam, and the design seems to have served him from the beginning of time. Birds make nests, and bees make honeycombs by instinct, and it seems to me there is no improvement necessary.

By contrast, men and women create, with the ability to take ideas, design products, and then construct them with the understanding that future generations will make them even better. The Wright brothers, working in their Dayton, Ohio bicycle shop, designed a flying machine that got Orville in the air for twelve seconds in Kitty Hawk. Sixty-six years later, another Ohioan, Neil Armstrong, walked on the moon.

The advances in communications are staggering. Time was when a kid—and that would be me—had to walk one mile to the Union Public Library and use the World Book encyclopedia to cobble together a report about the country of Bolivia. Today, a kid asks Google and in 0.62 seconds receives 604 million entries.

The day my mother died in 1997, I emailed Edith Hansen, the missionary to Indonesia I wrote about in a prior chapter. I sent her an email at midnight, and by the time I woke up the next morning, she had replied with a wonderful tribute to my mom. My father asked a reasonable question for someone born in 1917, who recalled how out-of-town calls meant long-distance charges, asked me "How much did that cost?" Nothing, I told him, though I did ignore the cost of the home computer and the monthly fee to the cable company.

The advancement of accumulated knowledge was recognized by Sir Isaac Newton, who famously said in 1695, "If I have seen further, it is by standing on the shoulders of giants."

Newton, considered one of the pillars of modern science, recognized he actually knew next to nothing. He knew that the laws of physics he identified only scratched the surface. "I don't know what I may seem to the world, but, as to myself, I seem to have been only like a boy playing on the seashore, and diverting myself in now and then, finding a smoother pebble or a prettier shell than ordinary, whilst the great ocean of truth lay all undiscovered before me."

Newton's thinking was inspired by his belief that God created the universe and did so in an orderly fashion. He wrote, "This most beautiful system of the sun, planets, and comets could only proceed from the counsel and dominion of an intelligent and powerful Being. This Being governs all things, not as the soul of the world, but as Lord over all; and on account of his dominion, he is wont to be called Lord God."

George Smith of the University of Missouri shared the Nobel Prize for chemistry for his work on the evolution of proteins.

"Very few research breakthroughs are novel. Virtually all of them build on what went on before," he told the Associated Press on October 3, 2018, the day the award was announced.

The doctors, nurses, and therapists who treated Leah spent years gaining knowledge passed down by those before them, studying volumes of accumulated information. They used equipment developed by former engineering students at places like MIT and CalTech, who used material not available a generation before them. Leah's diagnosis of a spinal cord stroke could not have been made without magnetic resonance imagining (MRI), according to Dr. Harvey Bennett, a specialist in child neurology and developmental medicine at the Goryeb Children's Hospital in Morristown who diagnosed Leah. Before the MRI, said Dr. Bennett, a diagnosis of a spinal cord stroke could have been made only during an autopsy.

The development of the MRI is credited to Raymond Damadian, who received the Lemelson-MIT Program's Lifetime Achievement Award in 2001 for his role in developing the noninvasive mapping of the human body.

Damadian, who died in 2022, was a Christ follower. He told *Guidepost* magazine, "How could a scientist achieve his goal of discovering the absolute truths that govern the natural world without the blessing of the Author of those truths? For me now the true thrill of science is the search to understand a small corner of God's grand design, and to lay the glory for such discoveries at the Grand Designer's feet."

What doctors once knew about the inside of a body was what they could learn by poking or cutting through the skin. Sophisticated medicine once featured bloodsucking leeches. Today doctors use x-rays, MRIs, blood work, and urine samples. They can map your DNA with a swab of your cheek. What doctors did not know about in Newton's time—and we are talking only four hundred years, a hiccup in time—were the presence of germs, viruses, DNA, and chromosomes.

At the beginning of the twentieth century, about one in ten babies who survived the birth process died before their first birthday. In 1950, according to the US Centers for Disease Control and Prevention (CDC), the death rate for babies in their first year was about one in fifty. By 2018, that figure was about one in two hundred, improving twentyfold since 1900.

In the twentieth century, men and women had accumulated knowledge about childhood illnesses and passed it on, leading to the dramatic decrease in infant mortality. In the early years of the century, diphtheria was a rabid killer of children, causing the deaths in 1915 of two daughters born to my grandparents.

According to the CDC, diphtheria is an infection caused by a strain of bacteria. It begins as a sore throat and causes a thick covering in the back of the throat. It can lead to difficulty breathing, heart failure, paralysis, and death. In Spain, diphtheria was called *garotillo*. Those who suffered died as if they had been strangled by a cord.

Diphtheria reached its peak in the United States in 1921 when 206,000 children were diagnosed and 15,520 died, according to an accumulation of state health department records. Then God's image bearers created a vaccine, and diphtheria has virtually vanished. Between 2004 and 2017, the CDC counted two cases. Polio was virtually eliminated in my lifetime when a vaccine was introduced.

Globally between three hundred million and five hundred million people died of smallpox in the first half of the twentieth century. Smallpox was virtually eliminated by a vaccine. I have a scar on my right shoulder to prove I was vaccinated, as did, I assume, everyone in my second-grade class.

During one of the COVID-19 peaks, I asked a woman if she

had been vaccinated. She said no. God was going to protect her. I was too polite to scream, "God already has! Men and women made in His image created a vaccine. It's all over the news."

"God did answer our prayers," said New York Governor Kathy Hochul, speaking at the Christian Cultural Center in Brooklyn on September 26, 2021. "He made the smartest men and women, the scientists, the doctors, the researchers—He made them come up with a vaccine. That is from God to us, and we must say, 'Thank You, God.'"

But where was God when children were dying of diphtheria, polio, and smallpox? Was God a lesser being, unable to answer the prayers of my grandmother in 1915 when her two daughters were dying?

No. He is unchangeable. It was men and women created in the image of God who accepted the challenge of curing and treating diseases. "Clearly Christians should allow God to develop them intellectually to the fullest extent," wrote James Montgomery Boice.

This is something only humans do. When mad cow disease ravaged Great Britain, with one thousand cases a week in 1993, not a single cow lifted a finger to find a cure. "Beasts haven't any art or technologies, scientific institutes or historical archives, philosophers or physicians," wrote Charles Colson. "Humans aren't like beasts; we've been created in the image and likeness of God."

William Lane Craig, a prominent Christian philosopher, responded to a question asked by a man devastated by the death of his mother from dementia. Craig suggested that when God created man in His image, He gave them curiosity to seek cures for such illnesses as dementia.

Craig wrote, "Perhaps God wants man to find cures for the diseases and infirmities that afflict us rather than constantly tinker with the world with miraculous interventions to cure people, just as He wants us to develop plumbers and electricians and computer scientists rather than magically solve our problems by constant miraculous interventions in the world, which would leave us like immature children rather than mature moral agents."

In an interview with the *Washington Post* published one year into the COVID-19 pandemic, Dr. Francis T. Collins, the director of the National Institute of Health, and a committed Christian, said, "God gave us both a sense of God's love and care and compassion, but He also gave us the brain and the opportunity to understand God's creation, which is Nature, which includes things like viruses.

"If we have the opportunity to heal through medicine, I think God expects us to do that and not count on some supernatural intervention to come and save us when He's already given us the chance to be saved by other means."

CHAPTER 27

He Did All Things Well

If Moses thought it was a daunting challenge to usher four hundred thousand men, women, and children through the Red Sea with Pharaoh's army in hot pursuit, it was small compared with the task God assigned Moses in the wilderness.

God wanted a tabernacle, an ark, a lampstand, priestly garments, and a breastplate ... and He wanted it all according to precise specs. "Make this tabernacle and all its furnishings exactly like the pattern I will show you" (Exodus 25:9).

The familiar menorah, a symbol to this day of the Jewish people, was to be made according to God's design. The cups were shaped like almond branches and to be hammered out of pure gold. The tabernacle was to have "10 curtains with finely twisted linen and blue, purple and scarlet yarn, with cherubim worked into them by a skilled craftsman" (Exodus 26:1). The ephod would have two onyx stones with the names of the sons of Israel engraved on the stones in the order of the sons' births.

The instructions for the craftsmen take up six chapters of the book of Exodus—as many chapters as the books of Galatians and Ephesians and 1 Timothy and more chapters than in the books of Philippians, Colossians, the two letters to the Thessalonians, 2 Timothy, Titus, Philemon, James, the two letters from Peter, three letters from John and one from Jude. The specs were that important.

What Moses now needed were craftsmen. That menorah, tabernacle, and ephod were not going to build themselves or drop like manna from heaven.

God gave Moses a man named Bezalel ben Uri and told Moses, "I have filled him with the Spirit of God, with skill, ability and the knowledge in all kinds of crafts- to make artistic designs for work in gold, silver and bronze, to cut and set stones to work in wood and to engage in all kinds of craftsmanship" (Exodus 31:3–5). God appointed Oholiab to help him. "Also, I have given skill to all the craftsmen to make everything I have commanded you."

The gift of artistry to Bezalel ben Uri is the first mention in the Bible of someone being filled with the Holy Spirit. He was not a priest, a teacher, a theologian, or a missionary. He was an artist.

In *Gleanings in Exodus*, Arthur W. Pink wrote, "Bezalel and Oholiab did not presume to intrude into this holy office of themselves, nor were they appointed by Moses, or by a committee made up of leading Levites, instead they were 'called' by God."

God put Leah in good places, at Morristown Medical Center and Children's Specialized Hospital in New Brunswick, where He had placed doctors and nurses and therapists with skills. The medical personnel may not have sensed a calling from God, like Bezalel and Oholiab, but it was God who framed them to have skills to develop to become healers.

In his book *Bezalel. Redeeming a Renegade Creation*, author Christ (rhymes with mist) John Otto noted that the Hebrew word *charash* is often translated "craftsman." The best modern equivalent, he suggested, is *artisan*. Quoting from one of his earlier books, Otto wrote, "The artisan is a renaissance person, able to do many things and create things of beauty. In the books of Kings and Chronicles, this term would be used to describe men sent by Hiram to build the Temple."

In *The Agony and The Ecstasy*, a biographical novel of the life of Michelangelo by Irving Stone, the author took liberty to suggest in the cool of the long afternoon of the seventh day of creation, God may have asked Himself, "Whom have I on Earth to speak for me? I had best create another species, one apart. I will call him 'artist.' His will be the task of bringing meaning and beauty to the world."

In *The Lords of Discipline*, novelist Pat Conroy tells the story of Will McLean, a student at Carolina Military Institute, a fictional school modeled after The Citadel in Charleston, South Carolina. One of Will's roommates lived in Charleston, and Will often visited the home of his roommate's mother, Abigail St. Croix. She believed in elegance, and her home reflected it.

> "I want to catch what you've got, Abigail," Will told her.
>
> "Catch what, Will?" she asked.
>
> "This thing you've got. The Beauty Disease. I want to spend my entire life perfecting the art of making everything around me as beautiful as possible. I want my furniture to be beautiful, my house to be beautiful, my gardens, my children, my wife … everywhere I look I want to be stunned by the sheer absolute force of physical beauty."
>
> "You're such a slob, Will," his roommate Tradd said with conviction. "You don't even

shine your shoes or keep your part of the room clean."

"Please tell your son to hush, Abigail," Will appealed.

Like Abigail St. Croix, Bezalel had the beauty disease. So did Michelangelo, Rembrandt and Beethoven.

On Carey Nieuwhof's Leadership Podcast aired on November 5, 2019, English theologian and Christian author N.T. Wright explained that he studied Latin and French at the age of eight and Greek at thirteen. "I didn't start Hebrew, sadly, until I was nineteen. Better late than never. I see those gifts, which I did not ask for but which I was given by God, and which I've been able then hopefully to use, and to use to help people.

"Some people are given extraordinary artistic gifts. They didn't ask for it, it just turns out that they can draw or paint or sculpt like nobody's business. If you've got those gifts, you've been given them for a purpose so that people like me who are not artists can have our eyes open to the dimensions of beauty, and indeed sorrow as well as joy, which the artist can draw our attention to."

I visited Leah in the hospital many times and drove her to outpatient physical therapy sessions at Children's Specialized Hospital in Mountainside. These people were medical artists.

In the spring of 2018, I had an appendectomy, with emergency surgery that began a few minutes after midnight, when my blood pressure was dangerously low (70-something). The surgeon removed my appendix, and the scar has since disappeared. Saving my life was a beautiful thing.

When we were young, our parents took us every summer to Aunt Maude's farm in Loganton, Pennsylvania. Aunt Maude lived there with my mother's cousin Jim Jenkins, a "pure mathematician," who spent time at the Institute for Advanced Study adjacent to Princeton University, the academic home of men like Albert Einstein, J. Robert Oppenheimer, and John Nash. The institute's motto is "Truth and Beauty." A movie about the life of John Nash is called *A Beautiful Mind*.

While he was in college, Jim told me, he had a choice between chemistry and mathematics. He chose mathematics. "With math, you could be more creative," he said.

When I built a free-standing garage, I hired someone to dig the trenches for the foundation, and I hired someone else to pour the concrete footings. My work began by laying a cinder block foundation that required four ninety-degree angles. I drew on high school geometry and applied the Pythagorean theorem, attributed to creative Greek thinker Pythagoras six centuries before the birth of Christ. A-squared plus B-squared equals C-squared. My foundation was perfectly squared. Truth and beauty.

During the COVID-19 pandemic, Perry L. Glanzer wrote in *Christianity Today*, "If epidemiologists, scientists and health care workers ignored God's call to study in college, they would have not been prepared to fight the virus. We need economists to help us navigate financial pitfalls. We need psychologists, poets, writers, philosophers to help us process the mixed emotions we feel. We need pastors, worship leaders and theologically equipped laypeople to help us see the pandemic in light of God's larger story."

Learning and applying skills is best served by a determined work ethic, wonderfully illustrated in a story told by Bruce Springsteen in his autobiography, *Born to Run*. The most recent of his E Street Band stadium concerts Donna and I attended lasted four hours and four minutes with no intermission.

Unless I blinked and missed it, Springsteen never left the stage. His work ethic is legendary.

Following the death of the band's saxophone player Clarence Clemons in 2011, Springsteen auditioned Clarence's nephew Jake Clemons as a potential replacement. Jake arrived late, and Springsteen was steaming. He had given Jake four or five songs to familiarize himself with. Jake said he "sort of" knew them. It was the wrong answer, met with Springsteen's anger. "Lesson number one: in the E Street Band we don't 'sort of' do … ANYTHING," wrote Springsteen.

Replacing Clarence Clemons is not a job but a "sacred position," said The Boss. "You don't DARE come in here and play this music for Bruce Springsteen without having your [stuff] DOWN COLD. You embarrass yourself and waste my time."

He told Jake Clemons to leave and not return until he had three solos down pat. "He called me a day or two later and said he was ready. When he came in this time, he was."

The Bible clearly teaches a work ethic. "Whatever you do, work at it with all your heart, as working for the Lord, not man" (Colossians 3:23). Nothing *sort of* about it.

As for the work of Bezalel and his artisans, the Bible tells us, "Moses inspected the work, and saw that they had done it just as the Lord had commanded. So Moses blessed them" (Exodus 39:43).

Thank God, the doctors, nurses, and respiratory therapists did not *sort of* connect Leah to a ventilator that morning in the ER. How many of us have visited a hospital and thought, as a medical professional does his or her job, *I couldn't do that. I'm not cut out for a job like this.*

The doctors, nurses, and therapists did all that for Leah, using God-given talent to heal.

CHAPTER 28

Diagnosing a Stroke

The night Abby brought Leah to the ER at the Morristown Medical Center, the staff had an extraordinary challenge—how to treat this otherwise healthy eight-year-old girl who suddenly could not move.

Heading the team of pediatric neurologists who would diagnose Leah was Dr. Harvey Bennett, a specialist in child neurology and developmental medicine, who performed what he called a "differential diagnosis. What it is and what it is not? We always suspected spinal cord involvement."

Initially, the team did not suspect a malfunction of the brain, a finding confirmed when an MRI of the brain was clean. If paralysis had been caused by trauma, her body would have shut down immediately, not gradually over twelve hours.

By the end of her first day, MRIs were done on her spinal cord, and, said Dr. Bennett, "We spent hours looking at her imaging." They came up empty. "Why is this happening to Leah? She is a perfectly healthy girl. Why is she different than the rest of the kids, who are athletic, doing cartwheels?"

One possibility considered was Guillain-Barré syndrome, a neurological disorder in which the body's immune system mistakenly attacks the nervous system outside the brain and spinal cord. That was ruled out early. Another possibility was transverse myelitis, an inflammation of the spinal cord. In the first few days of Leah's hospitalization, she was treated as if she had transverse myelitis. She was given immunotherapy drugs, steroids, and IVIG (intravenous immunoglobulin) drawn from donated blood.

"We threw the book at her," said Dr. Bennett, who spoke to former colleagues at Children's Hospital of Philadelphia (CHOP). "I remember them saying, 'You're doing what we would do.'"

The range of diagnosis eventually included the possibility of a spinal cord stroke, which occurs, explained Dr. Bennett, "when a fibrocartilage gets into very small vessels and clogs the vessels. That's what happened with Leah."

One reason for initially ruling out spinal cord stroke was its rarity. He remembered thinking, *It could be a stroke, but probably not, just on a statistical basis. The prognosis should be better than having had the demon of a stroke.*

By then, some of us had Googled "spinal cord stroke," and the findings were bleak. The National Institutes of Health (NIH) published a paper on spinal cord infarction of a young girl with no symptoms. It was a troubling read that portended a challenging future.

Case No. 1 was described as a "previously healthy 14-year-old female." According to the case report, she was in school and had difficulty breathing. She also had a burning sensation in her back, and when she went to the nurse's office, she vomited. Soon she lost sensation in her arms and legs. Breathing became even more difficult, and once hospitalized, she was placed on a ventilator. An MRI of her brain was normal. Through this portion of the NIH account, the story paralleled Leah's—pain, vomiting, difficulty breathing, paralysis, and normal brain function.

The story of Case No. 1 on the NIH website continued. Eighteen months after suffering the spinal cord stroke, she could turn her head and talk. She had minimal movement of her right hand. She was in a wheelchair and breathing with a ventilator. She suffered from anxiety and sleeplessness. Was this Leah's future?

When Leah was transferred to Children's Specialized Hospital in New Brunswick, her primary physician was Dr. Michele Fantasia, the hospital's director of the spinal cord injury program and a pediatric physiatrist. She had no experience to draw on. "I've been an attending physician here over twenty years, and I haven't seen anyone with a spinal cord stroke," she told me.

She explained how Leah's condition differed from a spinal cord injury, such as the one that instantly paralyzed Rutgers football player Eric LeGrand in a game at MetLife Stadium in 2010. "With a spinal cord injury like Eric LeGrand, you would have had something traumatic [to cause paralysis], none of which happened to Leah," said Dr. Fantasia.

Strokes occur mostly in people in my demographic. About 98 percent of strokes affect the brain and are often age related. Beginning at age fifty-five, a person's chances of suffering a stroke double every decade.

"Three of my grandparents had a [brain] stroke in a different season of life," said Dr. Beth Singer, the Hansen family's pediatrician, who knew Leah only as a healthy, vibrant kid who had suffered nothing more severe than a common cold. Working in her favor would be her youth, said Dr. Singer. "In an older person, perhaps they're going to have a heart attack and die. Leah's not going to have a heart attack and die. The parts of Leah's body are healthy. She has good lungs, a good heart. She has healthy young parts that can deal with this stress. What happened to Leah, I've never seen it in seventeen years, and I'll probably never see it again," said Dr. Singer.

The spinal cord is about eighteen inches long in an adult male and seventeen inches long in an adult female. It is about a half inch in diameter, protected by a tough coating called a dura mater and bones called vertebrae. It is well protected.

Any injury to the spinal cord is severe. By my reckoning, there are no minor spinal cord injuries, just major injuries and less-than-major injuries. According to the American Academy of Neurological Surgeons, between 250,000 and 450,000 persons in the United States have spinal cord injuries. When the spinal cord is severed, it is called complete, cutting off all signals from the body to the brain. The most common causes are vehicle accidents and gunshots.

Less common are spinal cord strokes. Unlike spinal cord injuries that occur in an instant, a spinal cord stroke can take hours or days before causing paralysis, when the spinal cord is gradually deprived of oxygen from the blood.

When Leah was in the second grade at Millington School, a man who has given inspirational talks around the world spoke at a school assembly. What Leah remembered was the man was in a wheelchair, and it was an assembly, and what kid doesn't welcome an assembly? Leah had no understanding that the man, Scott Chesney of Verona, New Jersey, had suffered a spinal cord stroke thirty-three years earlier. When Abby researched "spinal cord stroke," she found his story online, saw that he was in a wheelchair, and immediately closed the webpage.

Chesney suffered a spinal cord stroke on December 28, 1985, and the diagnosis eluded doctors until a retired pathologist from Africa, visiting Columbia Presbyterian Hospital in New York, examined an MRI, which was relatively new in the mid-80s. "Nowadays an MRI is the first thing [doctors] would do," Chesney told me.

At fifteen, Scott Chesney was the athlete every boy growing up in Verona wanted to be. He was the quarterback on the youth football team, point guard on his basketball team, and pitcher and shortstop on his baseball team.

On December 27, 1985, the Verona High School varsity basketball team was playing in a holiday tournament. The team trailed by ten points in the final quarter when Scott, then a sophomore, entered the game. "He created havoc for the other team," his older brother Bill recalled. Verona tied the game and then won in overtime.

The next morning when Scott woke up, his toe was numb. When he got out of bed, he took a step. "It was like my left foot wasn't there," he remembered. He had to ask Bill to do his paper route that Sunday—something he never had to do. The next day, Bill picked him up and carried him to the car and took him to the hospital.

When people ask Jay Mohr, a friend from their childhood together in Verona, what happened, Jay finds it difficult to explain, "He went to bed. Scott went to bed. Well, how did it happen? [Scott will say], 'I went to sleep.'"

When Scott Chesney had his spinal cord stroke, the paralysis gradually worked its way up from his toes. He and his family were concerned that paralysis would reach his brain and do untold damage. Fortunately, the paralysis stopped at his belly button. He would need a wheelchair for the rest of his life—though his disability has not prevented him from skydiving and surfing.

During inspirational speeches to schoolchildren, Scott does not focus on medical issues that kids would not understand. They just see the wheelchair. "I tell them, 'Dream, believe, work to achieve. Examine their own lives, and if you have challenges, there is a formula for them. Believe in yourself. Believe in your mission.'"

He has spoken to an estimated 1.5 million people in forty countries, including groups at the FBI, the Pentagon, sports teams, and grade schools like Millington School. He is an ambassador of the Christopher and Dana Reeve Foundation, and his story is told in *Ride the Wave*, a documentary released in the spring of 2020 that focuses, in part, on a team of supporters who help him surf.

As gifted an athlete as Scott was at fifteen, and Leah at eight, they would never be in a league with Pete Reed, an Olympic rower for Great Britain who won gold medals in Beijing in 2008, London in 2012, and Rio de Janeiro in 2016. The six-foot-six Reed was a member of the British Marines and was preparing to compete in the Tokyo Olympics when he announced on Instagram in October 2019 the "shocking news"—his words— that he had suffered a spinal cord stroke.

By one measure, he was gifted like no other person in the world. Google "largest lung capacity," and you will learn Pete Reed has a measured lung capacity of 11.68 liters. It is believed Olympic swimmer Michael Phelps has a lung capacity of twelve liters. The average adult male has a lung capacity of about six liters. The average adult female has less than five.

Reed once felt invincible. An interview with the London Times, published July 24, 2022, captured his thoughts as he looked forward to competing in the 2012 London Olympics. "Sitting there with oar in hand, Reed could not have been in a better state. Physically, this six-foot-six colossus of superhuman power and endurance had never felt stronger. Mentally he felt invincible. 'Forgive the apparent lack of humility' Reed says, 'but sitting on the start line, I felt sorry for the other boats.'

"Doctors can't be certain what caused my stroke. It was in the middle of my spine, so I'm currently paralyzed beneath my chest," he told his Instagram followers. "There is a very small chance I will make no recovery and very small chance I will make a full recovery. Much more likely it will be somewhere in between. All other news is great. My arms are still strong, and my brain is still as average as it ever was.

Reed had gone to the hospital on September 3, 2019, with pain in his chest and numbness in his legs. Three days later in the hospital, he felt pain like never before. "I could slowly feel it coming up through the legs and up to my chest. Within about 45 minutes the pain had gone up to my chest and I couldn't move."

Among the scores of visitors was Jurgen Grobler, his rowing coach. "Nobody knows my body better than Jurgen. He saw me at my physical best, so for him arriving to see me in a wheelchair was tough. He was the one person who I would try to impress physically, and it's a different world now."

Like Leah Hansen and Scott Chesney, athletics were a major part of his life. "There's nothing more beneficial to me now than my athlete mindset. Nothing," Reed told BBC Sport.

This mindset comes into play in recovery, said Dr. Singer. "Having a positive attitude, a feeling like you can achieve things, is good for your body, for your psyche. She could be 'Woe is me,' but Leah is 'Wow is me.'"

CHAPTER 29

Believe

Donna, Carrie, Abby, Peter, and I were at MetLife Stadium in the New Jersey Meadowlands on October 10, 2010, when the Rutgers University football team played Army. Rutgers had rallied from a fourteen-point deficit to tie the score at 17–17 with 5:16 remaining in the game. Rutgers' San San Te kicked off to Army's Malcolm Brown.

Rutgers' lineman Eric LeGrand headed in Brown's direction, eluding two Army players assigned to block him. "Instinct took over. Just before I exploded into him, one of my teammates dove for his legs. Brown responded by swiveling his hips and twisting ever so slightly as he reached the impact zone," LeGrand would write in his autobiography, *Believe. My Faith and the Tackle That Changed My Life.*

The impact between LeGrand and Brown was violent. Reporters from the *Star-Ledger* asked scientists to crunch the numbers. They measured Brown's speed at 20.45 miles per hour. The six-foot-two, 275-pound LeGrand ran toward him at 13.18 miles per hour. Their collision produced 833 pounds of force. "It was a perfect storm of size, speed and catastrophic misfortune," according to the newspaper. It was as if a world-class 150-pound sprinter ran into a brick wall at top speed. Brown suffered a broken collarbone. LeGrand's life changed in a moment.

LeGrand remained on the turf motionless. Medical staff from Rutgers and Army immediately tended to him. Rutgers head coach Greg Schiano, who feared the gravity of the injury, left Eric and ran toward the stands to retrieve Eric's mother, Karen.

Warren Bennett, a former football player and coach, and a partner of mine umpiring high school baseball games, remembered being at his home in Colonia, New Jersey watching the game on ESPN. He had known the young LeGrand as an active kid in the streets and playgrounds in Colonia. "When Eric was lying on the ground, I knew right away this was serious, real serious. As a former player, you know," said Bennett, who received scores of messages that day, seeking updates on Eric's condition.

Eric was gingerly placed onto a utility cart, and as the cart disappeared into a stadium tunnel, Bob Picozzi, who was calling the game for ESPN, said cautiously and hopefully, "They almost always turn out OK."

Almost always.

About once a decade, a high-profile player in the National Football League or on a major college team is paralyzed for life. Darryl Stingley of the New England Patriots in 1978. Marc Buoniconti of The Citadel in 1985. Mike Utley of the Detroit Lions in 1991. Eric LeGrand in 2010.

Rutgers defeated Army that day, 23–20, to improve its record to 4–2, though no one left the stadium enthused. The injury to LeGrand drained the energy from the program, and Rutgers lost the final six games of the 2010 season. Into the next season, the one question asked in the Rutgers football family was: how's Eric doing?

In the twelve years since, he would become an ambassador for Rutgers. No Rutgers football player will ever wear his No. 52. Before the fourth quarter at home games, the rock anthem "Don't Stop Believing" by Journey is played, and the camera is briefly trained on LeGrand, now a commentator on Rutgers radio broadcasts. In *Sports Illustrated*'s end-of-year issue in 2011, the cover photo, as chosen by readers, was of LeGrand being wheeled into Rutgers Stadium as a wet snow fell before the last game of the 2011 season.

I participated in *The Home News Tribune* coverage of the first few days of his injury, learning how National Football League stadiums are prepared for traumatic injuries. When the Buffalo Bills' Damar Hamlin suffered cardiac arrest in an NFL game in Cincinnati on January 2, 2023 he received immediate care from well-trained teams of first responders. (Watching that drama unfold live on ESPN I was reminded how it was Leah's good fortune – God's providence – that she was treated by well-trained professionals in the ER when she could no longer breathe. With both Leah and Damar Hamlin the risk from the loss of oxygen was immediate.)

Like Scott Chesney, LeGrand gives inspirational talks at area schools, including one he gave at Bernards Middle School, where my daughter Carrie teaches science. She spoke with him about that week's upcoming game at Michigan State but did not mention that she had been at the Army game. Why bring up the worst day of his life?

"No! No problem if you were there," Eric told me. "We've got a little history together, even though we didn't know each other. It was my last game. It's like you were there from day one. You didn't hear about it from somewhere else. You were in the stadium."

Until his injury, LeGrand explained, he had a casual faith

in God. As a freshman, he attended a Bible study led by John Maurer, who headed the Athletes in Action program at Rutgers. As a sophomore, he drifted away, with football and schoolwork demanding much of his time. Then came the tackle. God got his attention.

In his 2012 autobiography, he wrote, "God still cared about me, still had a plan for my life. He had not abandoned me on that football field. I decided that the greatest thing I had going was to trust in God's plan, whatever it was. If I could remain upbeat and positive in the face of such a devastating turn of events, then I would be doing everything God was asking of me."

He remembered his aunt Cheryl telling him, "Eric, everything that's happening is not for nothing. I don't believe this is just for you, this accident on the football field. I believe you have the opportunity to speak to people. To bless them with your words and bring attention to this type of spinal cord injury. I believe God has a purpose and a plan for you, just as he says in his Word."

Marc Buoniconti had lived on the wild side as a kid in Miami and said something similar in an interview with the *Miami Herald,* following the injury that left him paralyzed. "It's almost like God plucked me out of the air and said, 'All right, we're going to change the trajectory of your life. I'm not going to let you go down that path, and I'm going to offer you another opportunity to reveal the real you.'"

Malcolm Brown, the Army kick returner that day, is one of LeGrand's legion of admirers. He told the *Star-Ledger,* "Now I see that he's so positive, and it makes me feel a lot better. Obviously, we see now that he's been able to touch more lives just through all of his motivating people to get better and not just to lay down and accept defeat."

I mentioned to Eric how Leah's brother Joey, then six, had just started playing flag football, and his parents were skittish—a reasonable skittishness, considering what Leah was going through.

"Let the kids play," he said. "I am the person I am today because of football. You think football is running into each other and tackling. It's not just that. It teaches you how to deal with adversity. How to grow up to be a man, how to hold yourself accountable. How to hold people around you accountable. It gives you so many things you're going to need in life."

In 2012, LeGrand was inducted into the New Jersey Hall of Fame. On a recent trip to Newark Liberty International Airport, I saw a poster with his image and his testimony: "My life changed in an instant, but I will never look back and wonder 'What if' because I have been blessed with an opportunity to make a difference—to inspire the world—for all individuals—no matter their ability."

In the spring of 2022, the LeGrand Coffee House opened to great fanfare in downtown Woodbridge, with Coach Schiano, Woodbridge Mayor John E. McCormac, and New Jersey Governor Phil Murphy helping cut the ribbon. "Eric is a true inspiration, and I'm proud to watch him continue to spread hope and positivity—one cup of bELieve at a time," Murphy later tweeted.

Among the Rutgers athletes who visited Leah at Children's Specialized Hospital was Cole Murphy, a member of the 2018 football team. He said that one day Leah, then in a wheelchair, would be his guest and walk on the sideline before a home game. On October 26, 2019, before a game with Liberty University, she met Murphy, and he introduced her to several of his teammates.

LeGrand had invited us to the radio booth. There Leah met him, and Shaun O'Hara, a former Rutgers player who started for the Giants 2013 Super Bowl team, and former Rutgers quarterback Ray Lucas. O'Hara asked Leah if a particular movie was appropriate for his seven-year-old daughter. Lucas gave her his quick inspirational talk, explaining how he endured thirteen medical procedures on his knees and four operations on his neck. "The recovery all begins here," he said, pointing to his head. After the game, Murphy gave Leah the gloves he wore while holding the ball for five extra points and three field goals in a 44–34 Rutgers victory. Joey would claim the gloves and wear them to school in the next few winters.

When Schiano returned to Rutgers as coach in 2020, after having coached briefly in the National Football League, he said of LeGrand: "He's changed me as a coach, he's changed me as a man, and [his mother] Karen … the selfless approach she's taken is literally heroic. I've learned a lot from both of them, a lot. He has become a huge part of my life. I get choked up just talking about him. He is something, man. He is special."

Leah learning field hockey, Fall 2018

Leah and her siblings, Summer 2018

Leah's 10th birthday party, March 2019

Little League Opening Day, April 2019

Mrs. Jeni Clark with her 4 Hansens at Serena &
Joey's Kindergarten graduation, June 2019

Leah with Eric LeGrand, Fall 2019

Rick and Donna, Aunt Carrie, with Joey, Leah, and Serena, Summer 2021

CHAPTER 30

Samvincible

July 24, 2019, a Wednesday, was just another day at the beach at Ocean Grove, a section of Neptune Township founded as a Methodist campground in 1869. Ocean Grove calls itself "God's Square Mile." It's best known for the 118 tents set up every summer near the historic Great Auditorium, which has seats for six thousand, where President Theodore Roosevelt and evangelists Billy Sunday and Billy Graham have spoken, and where the Beach Boys and Tony Bennett performed.

Sixteen-year-old Sam Jarmer took to the beach as a kid. He was an avid surfer who became a lifeguard and was on duty that Wednesday. He took a break and, to cool off, ran to the ocean, dove in, and hit an unseen sandbar. His first instinct was to flip himself over to breathe. But he could not move.

It was Sam's good fortune that lifeguard Garth Greer saw what happened. It was as if Sam dove into a brick wall. His body went limp. When Greer reached him, he slid his arms under Sam's armpits and lifted him out of the water. With the help of five others, he placed Sam on a bodyboard, with his neck immobilized.

Sam's mother, Jessica Kilian Jarmer, was a few blocks away when her cell phone rang. "When I saw the name of his boss on caller ID, I knew there was a problem. I knew it was bad," she told me.

She began to run in her flip-flops toward Sam's beach when a man driving a golf cart on the boardwalk gave her a lift. When she arrived at the scene, she was told an ambulance was on the way. Sam was alert and able to talk to her. "I'm sorry, Mom. I'm so sorry, Mom."

The Jarmers—Jessica, her husband Scott and their three children—were scheduled to leave the next day for a vacation in Upstate New York. Sam realized the plans would be scrapped.

Jessica rode with Sam to Jersey Shore Medical Center, less than two miles away in Neptune. There he would undergo a six-hour surgery. While she was in a waiting room, a hospital employee came to sit next to her. Jessica wondered who she was. "I'm here for you," she remembered the woman saying. *Oh, my God. This is so bad they think I'm going to lose it.*

Sam, an athletic sixteen-year-old—surfer, skateboarder, Jet-Ski rider—had been counting down the days until he could get his driver's license. That day, he suffered an incomplete fracture of his C-6 vertebra. He would require a wheelchair for mobility and extensive therapy.

The Jarmers live a block away from the cottage Donna and I own in Ocean Grove. We have been close followers of Sam's progress, while Jessica has been a keen observer of Leah's. "I'm amazed whenever I see her riding her bike, knowing what happened to her."

Sam, in an instant, had suffered a traumatic injury, unlike Leah, whose body was gradually paralyzed over about twelve hours from the spinal cord stroke. Both are members of the community of people recovering from spinal cord injuries.

Dr. Michele Fantasia, director of the Spinal Cord Injury Program at Children's Specialized Hospital in New Brunswick, who was involved in both Leah's and Sam's care, explained how Sam's injury was "incomplete," which meant he had some motor and sensory function below the level of the injury. "As I say with all incomplete injuries, 'The sky's the limit.'"

Jessica is aware how fortunate Leah and Sam are to be alive today, what with advances in medicine. "I read where Elon Musk is getting involved in spinal cord research. I'm OK with that."

I mentioned to Jessica how I asked my cousin Butch—a hospital chaplain in Oklahoma City when a terrorist's bomb killed 168 people in 1995—"Where was God in Oklahoma City?" I told her his four-part answer: God weeps. Good people respond. We need a savior. God is God and in charge.

"Let me go right away to your fourth point," she said. "The way I look at it, we are God's children, made in His image. I have my children. If I want to keep them safe, I could put them in bubble wrap, stick them in a room, and feed them. And they wouldn't have any problems. But they'd have no life, no free will, no room to grow, to experience the world. But God gave us free will.

"What do we do as parents when our children are hurt? We pick them up, and we hold them. All through this experience with Sam, we have felt we were carried by God. Bad things are going to happen, like Oklahoma City, the World Trade Center. God's there to pick us up at the end. You know standing on a seesaw is a bad idea; it's not going to end well. The kid's going to do it anyway, but you're going there to take care of them."

Through it all, Jessica said she can count her blessings.

"Sam didn't drown. Sam didn't have any brain damage." She recalled how three days after the accident, Sam told his mother that he could have swallowed water, and rescue workers would have followed CPR protocol to save a drowning victim, tilting his neck back and doing additional damage to his spinal cord.

"Throughout all this, I have never been angry at God. I have always, always, always felt blessed," Jessica said.

Abby spent eighty-seven days and nights in Leah's hospital rooms in Morristown and New Brunswick. Jessica spent thirty-seven days and nights in Sam's hospital room in New Brunswick, afraid to leave because Sam could not press the red call button. "I didn't even know they had a Starbucks," she said. (Abby did.)

Not only did Jessica see God in all this, but she also saw the good in people, from the community, from friends, from strangers. The day after the accident, there was a prayer service at Thornley Chapel in Ocean Grove. Jessica did not attend so she would not have to answer any questions. That Friday, she attended a special Mass at St. Rose Roman Catholic Church in Belmar, with her son Michael and daughter Molly. She sat in the front row to avoid eye contact with those attending. Michael told her to turn around. The church was filled, and when they ran short on communion wafers, wafers were split in half.

A family friend contacted the New York Rangers, and when word spread around the National Hockey League, Sam received well wishes from scores of people in the hockey community. The New York Mets sent words of support. So too did people in the Hollywood community.

The most tangible gift to the family came from George Oliphant, host of *George to the Rescue,* which airs on NBC. When Sam returned from Children's Specialized Hospital, he moved into a cottage in Ocean Grove, across the street from the Jarmer house. Jessica's father lived in the cottage before his death in February 2019. The Jarmers had considered selling the cottage, but before his death, her father said, "Don't sell. You're going to need it someday."

Several people contacted Oliphant on the Jarmers' behalf, thinking he might be able to help them. At first, Jessica figured she did not qualify. "We had a place for Sam across the street. Then [Oliphant] said, 'I'd like you all to live together as a family.'"

Their house was not fit for Sam, however. The front portion of the house was constructed in 1881, with small doorways and a narrow staircase leading to the second and third floors. There was no way for Sam to maneuver while still in a wheelchair. The most innovative feature of the renovation was the construction of an elevator, to allow Sam access to his second-floor bedroom and to the third floor, where he could hang out with his brother and his friends.

Oliphant enlisted architect Paul Rugarber and interior designer Tracey Pearce, both of Point Pleasant Beach. Construction vans were a constant on our street during the renovation. Except for quick trips to her old kitchen to retrieve items, Jessica, Scott, and their children did not see the completed job until it was revealed to them by Oliphant and his team on October 18, 2020, with the cameras rolling. *George to the Rescue* aired two weeks later.

One of the strongest supporters of Sam has been Eric LeGrand, a brother of sorts. He posted a video on samvincible. com, a website that has chronicled Sam's recovery.

"Sam, it's your buddy, Eric LeGrand. Just want to reach out to you and let you know we got your back. You are not alone in this fight. I know you have great faith, great spirit, and great people around you, and always lean on those people because that's when you're going to need them the most, in these tough times, and they'll be there for you. Just like when you joined our family, a family you don't want to join, the spinal cord injury network. But when you're there, when you're in it for life, Sam, I'm always thinking about you. I'm always praying for you, my man. So stay blessed, stay positive, and be the inspiration that I try to be each and every day."

*Leah with her grandparents, Rick and Donna Malwitz,
at a Rutgers Football game, Fall 2021*

*Leah with her grandparents, Art and Ann Hansen, and
Aunt Sarah Hansen, at a cross country race, Fall 2021*

Leah in the musical "Matilda," Spring 2022

Leah with her Aunt Carrie (Malwitz) Walker, Fall 2018

CHAPTER 31

'Not My Will'

I n *The Lord's Anointed,* a novel published in 1935, author Ruth
Eleanor McKee told the story of twenty "soberly dressed"
adults about to set sail on October 23, 1819, from Boston to the
Sandwich Islands in the Pacific Ocean where they would preach
the Gospel. A most reluctant missionary was the unhappily
married Mercy Whitney. "It appalled her to think of spending
the rest of her life, provided she lived through the voyage, with
this dreamy scholar," wrote McKee. As the boat set sail on a
journey that would last 163 days, Mercy Whitney prayed, "Not
my will, but Thine will be done, and please make me not mind
so much."

On the first full day of Leah's hospitalization, Jon Coords,
now the pastor of One Church in Somerville, recalled praying,
"Asking for supernatural intervention, right there at that
moment, praying not my will but 'Thy will be done,' yielding
to God that He has a plan. He sees the full tapestry of what is
happening. You always have to have this kingdom mindset, this
eternal mindset."

In the familiar Lord's Prayer, Jesus taught us to pray to the
Father, "Your will be done." What we will all learn is that His
will is not always our will.

The collective will of our family certainly did not allow for a spinal cord stroke. One vision of the will that I had for Leah was how she would win the conference title in the girls' 400-meter race and go on to states. She inherited her mother's lean build and loping stride, and she seemed destined to glide to the state finals and a track scholarship. To God be the glory.

My will for Leah is not happening. And just like Mercy Whitney feared, I *did* mind when the events of March 5, 2018, occurred.

Since then?

I could not love Leah more than I do today. Or tomorrow. I love this version of what she has become. I love her story and want to pass it on, which is why I have written *Little Girl, Get Up.*

"When I was eight, I did not understand," Leah told Donna and me on the eve of her thirteenth birthday. "Looking back, God had a plan. He was with me. Everything worked out better than I can imagine."

The Bible says, "For I know the plans I have for you, declares the LORD, plans to prosper you and not to harm you, plans to give you hope and a future" (Jeremiah 29:11). This verse has been often hijacked by advocates of the so-called prosperity Gospel, who teach that we are to prosper with lush property, a Range Rover, and a robust portfolio. God does not promise that kind of prosperity.

He does promise suffering, however. That is His will. He also offers hope for the believer, based on His promise of our inheritance as a joint heir with Jesus. "My flesh and my heart may fail, but God is the strength of my heart and my portion forever" (Psalm 73:26).

How's she doing?

Leah entered her teen years a member of a vibrant youth

group at Millington Baptist Church, an excellent student at Central School, with a singing roles in spring musicals' *Matilda the Musical* and *Newsies*. On March 4, 2022, the day before the fourth anniversary of her spinal cord stroke, she went skiing at Gore Mountain in Upstate New York. In July, she returned to Tapawingo, the Christian girls' camp on Lake Pleasant, New York, this time accompanied by her friend Maggie Caputo.

"I'm not scared of the real world. I am very willing to do whatever I want, as long as Mom says it's OK. Mom pushes me to do everything."

She lives with two rambunctious younger brothers and a sister who's into gymnastics. "They're playing roughly, and I'm playing roughly with them. Honestly, I have a lot of fun. I try to be as normal as possible.

"Sometimes Timmy and Joey forget what my situation is, and my shoulder will pop out of joint. Dad will yell at the boys, and then he'll put my shoulder back. He's done that a few times." When her shoulder popped out of joint at camp, she instructed the nurse what to do.

"It's frustrating, having only one operating arm in a world built for two working arms. It is hard reaching for something over my head. But I like to think it was better that my upper body was affected [by the spinal cord stroke]. If it was the other way around and it was my lower body, I wouldn't be able to walk or stand up. I'd be in a wheelchair."

This was not lost on me on July 24, 2021. That day, our middle child, Carrie, married Josh Walker at the historic Raritan Inn in Califon, New Jersey. Seven of our eight grandchildren were in the wedding party, including Josh's two daughters from a previous marriage. (The eighth, Sarah Jeanne, not yet four months old, was excused.) The weather was a top-ten day.

The ceremony was held under a canopy of trees adjacent to

the South Branch of the Raritan River. To get to the ceremony from the tent where we would later have the reception meant a walk across grass of about the length of a football field. For some wedding guests, the walk was not possible. They waited under the tent for the ceremony to end.

When Scott Jones, the lead pastor of Jacob's Well, the church in North Brunswick where Carrie and Josh met, began talking, I was unexpectedly overcome with emotion. I could not stop crying—not exactly a bawling, sobbing cry that anyone would notice but an uncontrollable cry all the same. A happy cry.

The shortest verse in most translations of the Bible is John 11:35: "Jesus wept." The Aramaic Bible in Plain English converted those two words into seven: "And the tears of Yeshua were coming." That was me. The tears kept coming, though where I was sitting, the only one who could have noticed would have been Jones, and he was rightly focused on presiding at the marriage of Carrie and Josh.

I thought about Leah, about her not being in a wheelchair. There, but for the grace of God, the stroke could have affected her legs. But it didn't. She could walk across that grassy field.

Another blessing was how Leah matured into a beautiful and winsome young lady. Though she can be labeled handicapped, I somehow love this version of Leah even more. "This [spinal cord stroke] will not define Leah," said family friend Emily Caputo.

When hearing stories of others, including those of my cousin Pat, whose granddaughter died on her high school soccer field, or my former colleague Joe at the newspaper, whose son died in a car accident, or another former colleague whose grandson died in a motorcycle accident, I remind myself, *We have her.* Her life was restored that first morning in the ER. She survived the touch-and-go of that first week. When she asked her dad, "Am I going to die?" her dad said an optimistic, "Of course not."

201

That was half of it that day in July at the Raritan Inn. On this day, Carrie Malwitz, our second daughter, became Carrie Malwitz Walker.

Donna and I had been praying that Carrie would marry a man who loves Jesus as we do. Carrie and Josh met at church, where they are both active in the ministry. Josh comes from a strong Christian family. One small blessing of their story came in October 2020 when we went to the South Jersey home of Josh's parents, Bill and Deb Walker, meeting them for the first time. In the living room were several paintings that illustrated events in Jesus's ministry. One painting is of Jesus raising from the dead the daughter of the synagogue ruler, doing so with two Aramaic words: *Talitha Koum.*

That was on a Saturday night. Three days later, Deb died in her own bed, following years of pain. Today, when Carrie and Josh talk about his mother, we know her as the strong woman of faith whom we met over dinner in her home.

Carrie and Leah have an extraordinary relationship. (Carrie often borrows from Leah's middle name and calls her "Rosie.") Carrie told me how it was the Lord's timing that she met Josh after the crisis involving Leah had passed, knowing it would not have been easy to juggle her courtship with her devotion to Leah. And Leah was aware of what Carrie was doing during her three-month hospitalization and beyond. "She was our nanny," Leah said.

Four years after the stroke, Carrie said of Leah, "I could not possibly love her more, even though I wish with all my heart I could take all her pain away. I would have done anything to be the one in that hospital bed. But that wasn't God's plan. She inspires me in every way, and I just feel so privileged to watch her become who God wants her to be.

"I would have never written Leah's story this way, but I am

excited to see the end. And truly I never would have picked to be single as long as I was. But God is the author and perfecter of our faith. What a story He is writing. I just want to be a part of it."

When Leah was stricken, it was as if those four guys holding four corners of that discarded sail and lowering the paralytic man to Jesus got together and declared, "We got this." The family, the church, the local community, and the medical community acted collectively. We got this. Often I will ask Leah if she needs help, and she'll say, "No, I'm good." From four corners of that old sail, we say together, "No, we're good." We have all been blessed through Leah's illness.

Leah will sometimes be seen by people who had not seen her for a year or two. "I notice their jaws drop," said Leah. "Look at this girl. She's amazing."

On Memorial Day weekend 2022, to celebrate Leah's entrance into the teen years, Donna and I took Leah to Manhattan, first to Los Tacos, a family favorite for lunch; then to a Broadway musical, to the Gap in Times Square, to Krispy Kreme doughnuts, and to the Becco restaurant, another family favorite. For Donna and me, the hard part was keeping up with Leah's pace; she inherited speed-walking from her mother. "That," I would tell Leah several times into the next week, "was a perfect day." Even a fifteen-minute cloudburst made it memorable.

Who else had a perfect weekend? My cousin Pat Blank Egleston, whose granddaughter Julia Rose Potts was crowned Miss Rhode Island Teen USA, four years after Julie watched her sister Maddie collapse and die on a high school soccer field. Pat posted on Facebook, "We have always been proud of Julia, but never more than we were this weekend and not just because she won the title. We were extra proud because we understood what her competing in this pageant meant to her, and what it said about what she has overcome since 'that night.' No one deserved the joy she felt throughout this past weekend more than Our Julia Rose."

Our Julia Rose. Our Leah Rose. Quite the weekend.

Three months later Leah suffered a setback. Since 2008 our family has spent a week in the Outer Banks in North Carolina, skipping the year Abby was pregnant with the twins. On the final full day of our 2022 vacation Leah slipped on stairs, falling on her left shoulder. When she suffered her stroke four years earlier, I was twelve hundred miles away in Florida and did not see her for two days before driving though a rare March blizzard to reach home. My mind was fixed on the road. This time I was there, in the room where it happened. Timmy and I were playing pool in the basement when we heard her scream in pain. I saw her face and watched Peter comfort her, in real time. I would trace Abby's movement on my smartphone when Peter drove ninety minutes to the ER at the hospital in Kitty Hawk. A little after midnight she returned and managed a smile. For the next few weeks, I would see her get up, again and again.

Leah, who had dislocated her shoulder, broke a bone and tore ligaments, could have stayed home from school, but was fixed on going, with an aide pushing her in a wheelchair through the hall to prevent her from being jostled. (Jostling in middle school hallways seems to be a thing.) After a few weeks she abandoned the wheelchair. Allowing for the difficulty of playing the trombone she began playing the baritone. She was then seen by a fresh set of physicians, including two who work with the New York Football Giants. She is a normal teenager, with a large group of friends and a spirit of adventure. Her story is still in the beginner stage and keeps getting better.

When I was a teenager at the CMA church in Union, our

pastor, Rev. Robert Clancy, an important figure in my spiritual development, walked the young peoples' group through the Westminster Shorter Catechism of Faith, assembled by the Church of Scotland in 1648. It begins with the question: "What is the chief end of man?" The answer: "Man's chief end is to glorify God, and to enjoy Him forever."

My prayer is that this book gives glory to God by telling the story of Leah's recovery from a spinal cord stroke, and the stories of her helpers from four corners. My prayer is that this book gives glory to God, knowing that those who believe Jesus healed us at the cross will enjoy Him forever.

There is a story in Matthew 20, about the owner of a vineyard who hired workers at dawn, He hired another crew at nine, another at noon, another at three, and another at seven, promising them all one denarius. At the end of the day, the crew hired at dawn protested. *This isn't fair.* They worked all day, while the crew hired at seven worked only an hour. "Don't I have the right to do what I want with my own money?" said the owner of the vineyard. "Or are you envious because I am generous?"

What this parable tells me is that when people in my current demographic accept Christ's invitation they will get the reward of heaven, just like that eight-year-old boy who walked the aisle when Billy Graham spoke in Ocean Grove in 1956, believing in the Lord Jesus Christ.

In a sermon Dr. David Martyn-Lloyd Jones preached in 1954 at London's historic Westminster Chapel, he asked, "Are you a child of God? The only condition is the utter, absolute recognition of your desperate, helpless need and of what He has done and what He can do for you and in you—what He will do if you but ask Him to do it. Ask Him now."

Leah after a week at Camp Tapawingo, Summer 2021

Leah and her mom Abby, Summer 2021

Leah and her mom Abby, Fall 2021

The Hansen Family, Summer 2021

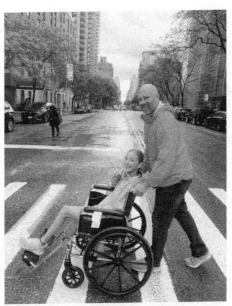

Leah and her dad Peter in New York City for a doctor's visit, Fall 2022

Leah's Children's Miracle Network of Hospital's
"Miracle Child" photo, Summer 2021

GRATITUDE

When Donna and I were married, we pledged to stay united, "from this day forward, for better or worse." Our wedding ceremony ended with the Fanny J. Crosby classic hymn, "To God Be the Glory." Our life together has been filled with many *betters*. The births of three children, the weddings, the grandchildren, vacations. We were blessed abundantly. Then came the *or worse*, when our oldest grandchild suffered a spinal cord stroke at the age of eight. We would walk through this together and walk through the writing of this book together. Donna's contributions cannot be properly measured. Nor, can the contributions of Abby and Peter. Who modeled their Christian faith through their daughter's challenges.

Thank you to our family, beginning with Peter's parents' Art and Ann, Leah's aunts Carrie, Sarah, Deborah and two named Elizabeth, and Uncle Andrew, who is affectionately called "Uncle Ohno," a name given by an infant Leah. It was Andrew whose technical skill helped this author, who was raised on manual typewriters. Thanks to my siblings Nelson, Alieta, Dan and Ginny, and my cousins Elaine Malwitz Thomas, Elise Malwitz Henrichs, Edna Malwitz Russo, and cousins Ken Blank, and Pat Blank Egleston. (Butch and Sis). Ten of us grew up together as neighbors on Vauxhall Road in Union, attended Hamilton School in waves and knew the blessings of family.

Bill Zapcic, a friend from my newspaper days and avid follower of the *Associated Press Stylebook*, was a valued editor. So, too, was Dave Lieberfarb, a colleague on the *Rutgers Daily Targum, and* Lori Granato Sica, whose editing and comments were a source of encouragement.

The people of Liquid Church did what New Testament churches are supposed to do, including Tim Lucas, Sara Gill, Peter Pendell, Aimee Pendell Huber, Jon Coords, Mike Leahy, Kayra Montanez, Keri Dolbier, Kristin Smerillo, Maria Scholma and Jan and Jeff Allen, who headed the crew of Ryan Smerillo, Josh Gill, Drew Huber, and Tim Scholma to restore the Leah Tree to health, during the first week of her hospitalization. Thanks also to members of the universal church, Dr. Gregg Haag, Linda Haag, Jonathan Schaeffer, Mark Kincade, Perry L. Glanzer, Bob Grahmann, Edith Hansen and Joe Hofmann.

Thank you to the many prayer warriors, beginning with Dr. Thomas and Sally Padhi. Soon after I left the newspaper business Dr. Padhi asked, "When are you going to write your book?" (Here it is.) On the day Abby and I did a final read of this manuscript, our pastor Mark Kincade emailed the Grace Alliance Church congregation at 8.43 p.m. "Dr. Padhi went to be with the Lord an hour ago."

It was easy to get Leah's school teachers and administrators to talk gushingly about her, including Jenifer Clark, Jen Tremarco, Noelle Milito, Jennifer Dawson, Beth Fischer, Karen Freeman, and Maura Aimette. The same could be said for people in the community, beginning with Jaime Falvey, who deserves special mention for her role as coach and organizer of a GoFundMe campaign. Others include Jeff Wanamaker, Tim Simo, Darcy Carn, Aubrey Eline, Lisa Scanlon and Jon and Dawn Seccamanie. Those in the community who told important stories include Long Hill Police Chief Ahmed Naga, Bob English, Mary Ann DeFinis, Scott Lavender, and Joe Shaw.

Thanks to the Helpers, members of the medical community, including Dr. Harvey Bennett, Dr. Michelle Fantasia, Dr. Steven Kirshblum, Dr. Beth Singer, Dr. Erin Johnson, Julie Connelly, Shannon Silverstein, Philip Salerno, Elaine Andrecovich, and Megan Granozio.

Thank you to Concierge Hanna Nate and the staff at WestBow Press for assisting in the publication of *Little Girl, Get Up*. Thanks to the readers and, as Leah whispered on a video during her first week in the hospital, "Thank you for praying."

Writing for the newspaper, my deadline was typically about six o'clock for a daily story or Thursday noon for a Sunday piece. In writing *Little Girl, Get Up*, the deadline was all mine. I did not know when to stop because the story kept getting better.

Soli Deo Gloria.